Representation of Women Space

REPRESENTATION OF WOMEN SPACE

(Vol. I)

Edited by

Bratati Dey

KUNAL BOOKS

New Delhi-110002 , India

KUNAL BOOKS
4648/21, 1st Floor, Ansari Road,
Daryaganj, New Delhi-110002
Phones: 9811043697, 011-23275069
E-mail: *kunalbooks@gmail.com*
Website: *www.kunalbooks.in*

Representation of Women Space

First Published 2018
ISBN:978-93-86714-42-8

Cover Credit: A detail from a Mithila Painting

Published in India by Prem Singh Bisht for Kunal Books, and printed at **Milan Enterprises**, Delhi.

Dedicated to

My parents

Their care to be with knowledge

ACKNOWLEDGEMENTS

My heartfelt thanks to Dr. Nilanjana Das (Associate Professor and Head, Department of Geography, University of Calcutta) my philosopher and guide for her loving support and encouragement. Thanks to my friend Abhijit Goswami for his consistent support. Thanks to all the authors in this book for contributing the article of their research work. I wish to thanks research scholar of the University of Calcutta, my colleagues of Dhruba Chand Halder College and my friends forever. Express my sincere thanks to the contributors who kindly accepted our request to include their opinion and rendered necessary information, assistance and cooperation during the compilation of this volume. I wish to pass on my sincere thanks to many scholars worldwide whose valuable works have been consulted and drawn upon during the compilation of works. The blessings of information technology are highly acknowledged through which much information, data and study materials are gathered.

I am deeply obliged to Mr Prem Singh Bisht of Kunal Books New Delhi for accepting the manuscripts and bringing out this volume in a short period and in graceful manner.

PREFACE

This book is an outcome of authors' participation and contribution of original articles on women space in society. Here women space denotes mainly tangible and intangible space of women in society. The subject of women and representation of its space in society encompasses a variety of issues and topics. Theoretical framework includes all representation of time and space. Feminist geographers have proposed how space is a complex web of relations of domination and subordination, a "power-geometry" of difference. While feminist and postcolonial theories explore notions of nomad identity, exile, hybridity and marginality, maps of postmodern social space elaborate the politics of representation in terms of the "geopolitics of location" (McDowell). The web of power that constructs everyday life is spatialized, and women are both actively and passively influenced by space in their constructions of identity. Segregated space has been described variously in binary terms of material/social, geographic/cultural, metaphorical/actual, real/symbolic, and real/nonreal. As Gillian Rose elaborates, the difference between real and non-real spaces is constructed through terms of sexual difference. Thus the coincidence between material, symbolic and discursive constructions of space influence and determine the gendered construction of space versus non-space in social, spatial and metaphoric terms. This book problematizes concepts of female space by way of two directions from tangible and intangible world. It analyzes representations of the role of women in terms of the "traditional" place of woman in the society. In this book *Real and Imagined Women*, has been delineates how in the context of women negotiations of identity, agency and even daily safety revolve around conflicts between the state and feminism, and between tradition and modernity. While the Hindu and Muslim veiled woman may respectively appear to be a relic of traditional class and religious values, or an icon of the eroticized female body of colonial desire, despite the impact of modernization/globalization, she still appears as a powerful – and ambiguous – indicator of meaning. Theoretical approaches (as well as the media) in the Western world have focused on the linear women space in the society, where women and their problem are categorized in same manner, although, as analyzed here, the regional material and cultural space are subdivided. The gendered space of women that has been theorized as delineating and enforcing an inside/outside, private/public, female/male dichotomy, is an extreme form of sex role differentiation that contentiously provides both "separate worlds and symbolic shelter" (Lateef 133). As Gayatri Chakravorti Spivak points out in her famous essay "Can the Subaltern Speak?" the voice of subaltern woman remains silent and irreclaimable. Yet how far is the figure of Indian woman also invisible as well as silent? In contrast to an American based feminist writer such as Spivak, who regards the power of speech as synonymous with agency, Jung suggests that "silence could be a language through which women in this land realized themselves". This book has mainly dived into two parts one that is deals with tangible and material space of women. Another part deals with intangible and cultural space of women. In both ways this book tries to understand the women in representation and representation of women in society. Later, women space concept has been widely discuss in brief manners.

This book includes five articles in first section. First article is on situating women in Geography: An Indian perspective authors Taruna Bansal and Awadh Narayan Choubey has examined the ways in which the spaces for women have been constructed in geography keeping the academic and scientific communities. The first part of the article deals with the demographic composition of geography in India and how women are placed in this discipline. Here the study is based on Central Universities (approximately 30) with Geography as a masters and research programme.

In second article author Arundhati Bhattacharyya has focused on migration space of women. She tries to establish that women are often looked at as non-subjects. The patriarchal State have, at times, provided step motherly treatment to women migrants. Traditionally, the identity and citizenship of a woman was totally dependent on the father or the husband. The women and the children are the worst sufferers, in such process of forced migration. Evidences are found among Rohingya refugees, Chakma refugees, Tamil refugees, refugees from Syria, Afghanistan and those who are forced to leave their own country. International instruments provide guidelines regarding treatment of migrants. There is need to protect the rights of the migrants in all countries, in every situation to have a peaceful and egalitarian global society. This paper has projected a glimpse of travails of travels.

Authors Nirupama Patwardhan and Shubhasheesh Bhattacharya try to focus on the working space of women in India. They focus on that working women in India face a challenging set of obstacles both at home and at work and coupled with for the most part, negative gender role perceptions, hinders their socio-economic status and prevents equal participation in the workforce. The Government and society in general as well as organisations have a significant and vital role to play in the development and promotion of women in the economy and the social order. Bridging the gender gap for working women in India would lead to huge economic upturns for the country. However, for this to occur a paradigm shift in the way women and their roles are perceived is imperative. Only then will India be able to claim a place as a progressive and leading nation of the world.

In next article Shelly De (Pandit) tries to discuss about women space on empowerment and entrepreneurship. She emphasis on that Women empowerment is concerned with the gaining of autonomy and control over resources, which includes many dimensions such as economic, social and political. As entrepreneurs, women have to take firm decisions to run the organisation smoothly. The decision taking powers integrate their needs for empowerment and motives for empowerment which is directly related to their economic and social status. She has done this article in a case study manner where she focused that SMGULP is a women's organisation manufacturing various products from Papad, Appalam, Masala to Detergent. Remuneration is the same for everyone, and profits and losses are shared equally among the member sisters, so there is no possibility of concentration of assets and wealth. Lijjat refuses to accept donations, but instead provides donations to the needy. The entrepreneurial success of the organisation is based on Gandhian philosophy of Sarvodaya and from the efforts of its member sisters who have withstood several hardships with unshakable belief in 'the strength of a woman'. The members are now economically and socially enough empowered to realize their full identity and power in all spheres of life.

In next article Saswati Ghosh has focused on internal migration space of women. Where she look into the internal migrant women, how the responsibility of social reproduction is being outsourced to the 'other' women by society in general, but without recognizing them as workers. Apart from that, it will also look in to the internal migrant women as a distinct category in the labour market, causes and consequences of their migration, definition and extent in India, the push and pull factors, the areas of concentration and "otherisation" of these women in the process, with the denial of political, economic and social rights, often along with apprehensions and allegations of criminal activities often attached with them. As their numbers is expected to rise, specific policy framing becomes imperative to recognise and protect them as workers.

This book includes five articles in second section. First article has written by Shreya Mukherjee on photographic spaces of women in studio. This article aims to investigate the visual aesthetic paradigms practice by the Indian photographers in representing women, during the pre-digital era, in the photographic studio spaces. The transforming time and differing strata of class gets mirrored in the photographs of the era. The confined spaces of studios echo the bounded spaces of the private zones of houses, blurring the difference between the private and public. Reading through the photographic framed spaces one tends to venture into sub-layers of undefined, unheard stories. The photographs of women, some of which, once for private viewership now move into a public eye opening up avenues to re-read them in varying context and the others which were meant for public viewing extends fresh meanings. The photographers like Ahmed Ali Khan, Abbass Ali, Sawai Ram Singh II Maharaja of Jaipur, Maharaja of Tripura Bir Chandra Manikya are few of the well known names who add images to this genre of photography. The photographic studio's provided a space were the women managed to be immortal, willingly or unwillingly, through not expressing the inner true selves but by being the part of larger visual, unheard histories.

Lopamudra Maitra Bajpai has focused on women space in literature. She emphasis on the the role of women in Bengali oral traditions and folk tales has been of significant discussion across several publications. The many voices echoed through the stories often speak of the several woes faced by women at various and different stages of life. The collection of *Thakurmar Jhuli* (Grandmother's Bag of Tales) is a collection of very similar folktales from Bengal (undivided Bengal and before the Indian independence- followed by the partition of 1947- encompassing the present state of West Bengal in India and the neighbouring country of Bangladesh) is a most popular collection first published by under the efforts of Dakkhinaranjan Mitra Majumdar. A collection of floating, oral folktales from West Bengal, the book was first published in 1907. Best loved stories of fairies, demons, princes, and princesses- and each story has a central focus on women- voicing various concerns, anxieties and happiness of women. Each voice of women however exudes an essence of a secondary role in society and a tone of woe. However, amidst the stories of *Thakurmar Jhuli* is the story of *Kironmala*. This folktale of *Kironmala*speaks of a story of a 'homely and dutiful', yet a 'brave princess who battles all evil to save her two brothers and her kingdom'- finally reuniting with their log-lost father- the king. Over the years, the story has been transcribed (published as a part of a book) and also adapted across various audio-visual formats (across the last few decades). However, a significant aspect to note is the remoulding of *Kironmala*- breaking away from the other stories from the collection of *Thakurmar Jhuli*- where the voice of women follow a typical pattern. The story of *Kironmala* speaks of changing times within its patriarchal mould. This paper looks into the original folktale and its format and how it has evolved over the years- incorporating changing roles of the female lead character-*Kironmala*. The paper attempts to highlight a 'voice'- breaking away from the standard pattern and evolving to create a niche for representing itself amidst a global world through the world of popular culture.

In next article Md. Iqbal Sultan focuses on women cultural space in Bengali travelogue. He describes that Bengali travelogues written by women are few in number, specially on abroad or foreign countries. In present study two such travelogues have been taken into consideration. The first one is 'Bongomohilar Japan Yatra'(1915) by Hariprava Takeda and the second one is Priti Sanyal's 'Farasi Desh Anyo Chokhey'(1998). Coincidentally, both the books are first travel writings on Japan and France by Bengali women travellers. Hariprava Takeda sketched society and culture of Japan through the eyes of a house wife. On the contrary, Priti Sanyal dwelled in France almost two decades with her husband for profession. She also narrated lifestyle, culture and different issues of contemporary urban society. Both the authors described a lot about 'Cultural Space' but their view was different. In spite of different approaches, both the books have revealed themselves as a conclusive geographical document of the respective regions.

In next article Samahita Chowdhuri discusses on cultural space of women in society. She discuss on the women and Hinduism in perspective of Indian society. The spirituality dominance over religious belief has transformed to raise the present day modern religion. Such transformation has taken a long path. Maintaining hierarchies of domination and oppression in different parts of the world in various ways, religions are playing active role. This paper reveals the women's' status in Hinduism. Varieties of images of women are there in Hindu epics and scriptures. In reality, the Hindu ideal is gender balanced with man as the creator and women as the lover.

In last article describes the space of women in Vedic period in India. This paper tries to explore the historical evidences which reconstruct the women space at this period.

Bratati Dey

List of Tables and Figures

List of Tables and Figures

Contents

Contents

Section I

1

Situating Women in Geography: An Indian Perspective

Taruna Bansal & Awadh Narayan Choubey

Abstract

Geography as a discipline has undergone a process of re-writing over the last few decades and the most noticeable change in the nature of the subject has been the introduction of women and gender studies. But the area for concern is that in spite of these developments the discipline continues to isolate and exclude women in the academic and scientific communities. This argument of mine can be complemented by the insignificant number of women in the profession of academic geography in comparison to other social sciences. The studies done in this regard suggest that there has been overwhelming male composition in geography in the past which is continuing to the present. Even in its demographic composition the discipline has been masculine in nature.

The present article examines the ways in which the spaces for women have been constructed in geography keeping the above background in view. The first part of the article deals with the demographic composition of geography in India and how women are placed in this discipline. Here the study is based on Central Universities (approximately 30) with Geography as a Masters and Bachelors Programme.

Introduction

Geography as with most disciplines is undergoing the process of re-writing and the most noticeable change in the nature of the subject has been the increased visibility of feminist approaches in geography. In other words, geography is being rewritten with women in the focus now and this process has produced an assortment of literature with diverse theoretical perspectives.[1] But before we discuss the concerns of feminist or gender geography we must bring into notice that patriarchal structures do not possess their own lives rather they persist because they have been institutionalized and reproduced by countless opinions, judgments and actions of many actors.[2] Many attempts have been made by feminist geographers to understand the interplay of human agency and structures with inclusion of women in them but still it remains an unexplored area when it comes to the discipline itself. If one thinks about the histories of women's employment in Geography one has to answer two questions- one where they have been present and where they have been absent (Monk, 2004).

The women's status in geography as a discipline imitates the masculine orientations and the most important concern of the Feminist geographers have been how space and place have been constructed within the philosophical foundations of geography implicating gender within those constructions (Staeheli and Martin, 2000). To start with, if we try to theorize geography as part of cultural creation, then it is but obvious that it will bear the impression of that culture. If a society is patriarchal, so will be its geography. This is a deceptively the most simplistic summary of the progression of geographical thought over the period of time. In fact, the idea of gendered geography is very new and very radical. It has nurtured itself on the basis of feminist thoughts which grew from ideas generated by the women's liberation movement during the 1970s.[3]

From its inception, a crucial feature of feminist geography has been its ability of scholarly cross-fertilization and multi-disciplinarity.[4] And, to appreciate this theoretical capability of feminist research in geography, one has to understand the two underlying themes on which the entire feminist scholarship is based. Firstly, feminist research is not just about women rather it is about how women form an essential part of the human-environment relations. Secondly, it is not an empirical study, rather a process of methodological and conceptual modification of addressing the issues of women in geography (Hayford, 1974; Mackenzie, 1984; Hanson, 1992; Rose, 1993; Massey, 1994; McDowell, 1997; Oberhauser, 2000). In the words of McDowell and Sharp (1997), *'the major goal of feminist geography is to investigate, make visible and challenge the relationships between gender divisions and spatial divisions, to uncover their mutual constitution and problematise their apparent naturalness'*.[5]

Not surprisingly, the nature of geographical research echoes the themes persistent in the larger universe of feminist theory and inquiry. Within the discipline, some research do focus on the "geography of women," – interpreting that the world of women is different from the world of men; some of it even extends the methodical borders of the discipline by introducing gender as a category of explanation and theory; and some examines the disadvantages to women of living in a world designed by patriarchy. Whatever the case may be one area which draws attention is the invisibility of women in traditional geographical studies and theories. Trivers (1978) draws attention to the main foci that women have been denied place in geography. The discipline has been male dominated and one cannot find an answer to that question that just how many women geographers are there in universities across the world.

The present article examines the methods in which the spaces for women have been build upon in geography keeping the above background in view. The first part of the article deals with the review of feminist approaches in geography. The second section deals with the academic discipline of geography and how women are placed in this discipline with special reference to India. The third section of the paper deals with the methodological issues and how geography can be made more humanistic by not excluding the other half of the human population in the broader field of human geography. Conclusions are presented in the last section.

Feminist Approaches in Geography

The history of Geography clearly outlines that the discipline developed as a field of study with its roots in explorations and discoveries during the middle ages. Most of the geographic societies around the world were founded to publicize information and knowledge gathered by the explorers. The basic philosophy of the discipline was to codify and systemize knowledge gathered mainly through fieldwork which was considered inaccessible and unsafe. As a result, this academic discipline has been conquered by men. Some women did make an attempt but the knowledge generated by these was not usually included into the more formal knowledge base or theoretical foundations of the discipline (Domosh 1991). When women entered the academics of geography they were often concentrated in the area of geography education that is either in training teachers or working as tutors in different schools and colleges (Monk 1998). These developments though slow, made a significant influence on geography as now Feminist geography, clearly became part of the thick braid of geographic research. This discipline now celebrated what feminism calls for. It started making spaces for women and feminism within the discipline (Staeheli and Martin, 2000).

Like all the fields of geography, feminist geography has developed in a social and political context that influenced the themes selected for and analysis and the methods adopted to investigate them.[6] The sub-discipline encompasses two areas of discourse –geography and

feminism – which further include diversified approaches. But when geography embraced feminist scholarship, it provided the later with its approaches to study the concerned subject matter. Hence emerged the geography of gender embedded within the conventional geographic paradigms. This was dominated by ideas based on feminist theories on how to explore the relationships between gender and geographies; and how eventually they have structured and transformed themselves mutually (Pratt, 2000).[7] In simpler terms, it looks into the geographical debate about women's position, the social construction of gender identities and changes in gender divisions over space and time.

For further understanding of the concerns of feminist geography one has to undergo a historical survey of the area starting from its inception in 1970s. During the mid-seventies period of time the geographers engaged in this field were trying to create '*geography of women*'. The main purpose here was to document systematically how women were disadvantaged in many spheres of life. This added women to the ground of geography both as producers as well as subjects of knowledge and analysis. The earliest feminist works in geography paid attention to map the constrains women face in differential spaces (Davies and Fowler, 1971; Hayford, 1974; Tivers, 1977; Ardener, 1981; Monk and Hanson, 1982). The studies were strongly influenced by radical and welfare approaches.

The foundation for many subfields and interests as new theoretical constructs was laid in the 1980s. These introduced the studies which highlighted the role of gender as an influential tool and an explanation instrument in geographical processes. Now the studies were focused on the geographical inquiry of gendered spatial divisions between public and private, particularly in the sphere of work and urban processes (Zelinsky, 1982; Christopheson, 1983; Rossini, 1983; Massey, 1984; Monk, 1984; Mackenzie, 1986, Nelson, 1986; Pratt and Hanson, 1988). It was during this decade only that the first cooperative study was published as *Geography and Women* in 1984 by the Women and Geography Study Group of the Institute of British Geographers. This was a sustained effort at outlining the critique of human geography and an alternative feminist approach. For the point of view of study group, feminist geography looks at how socially created gender structures form and transform space in a project dedicated to ending gender inequalities through social change.[8] They chose four streams of feminist approaches which were to be included in mainstream geography. These were (i) feminist urban geography (ii) women's increased participation in the public sphere (iii) separation between home and waged work and (iv) women's activity in changing the developing world.

Feminist geographers thus, not only acknowledged gender divisions and the inequalities in women's position both in the developed and developing countries but also started explaining the patterns of gender inequality. The main source of these works were rooted in the literature from feminism rather than from geography; as a result, the sub-discipline started moving towards a feminist geography rather than a geography of women which require areas of everyday life and of the academic literature that usually are not regarded as geographical.[9] They addressed the issues of the negligence of women, challenged falsifications about women and argued that gender has emerged as the axis of social discrimination and segregation in geographical research.[10]

In the decade of nineties, the feminist geography moved further and opened up enquiries about ways in which spaces and places were segregated in terms of the experiences of different people of different groups (Nairn, 1997; Burgess, 1998; Longhurst, 2001). This feminist geography thus started rethinking gender and its relationship to space and place. The major proponents of this approach were Doreen Massey and Gillian Rose.

Massey analyzed the dynamic relationship between class (in terms of social relations) and production (in terms of spatial organization); thus conceptualized the interrelations linking space, place and gender. Rose's interpretation of this relationship differs from that of Massey's. She analyses this association in terms of challenges become daily experiences of women.[11]

In recent years, the feminist geographers thus got actively engaged in deliberations that questioned both the unity/singularity of knowledge and the subject of 'woman'. As a result, a rich literature surfaced on sexuality and gender and the way they perform in different spaces. Moreover, the scope of feminist geography broadened as the feminist geographers started contributing in different fields of geography like economic and labour geography (McDowell and Graham, 1996; Friedberg, 2001), political geography (Staehcli, 1996; Secor, 2001), urban geography (Gilbert, 1997; Bondi, 1998), cultural geography (Katz and Monk, 1993; Anderson, 1996) and many more.[12]

The above discussion clearly shows four basic themes of feminist geography which emerge and re-emerge to distinguish it as a field of study. First, feminist geography is closely related with political movements and analyzes them. Second, it is an interdisciplinary subfield. Although its roots are grounded in the radical literature, it has engaged itself in major theoretical approaches of geography like in political and cultural geography, in urban and environment research, in the literature on economics and migration as well as in the writings dealing with methodological issues. Third, this subfield studies the relationship between space, place and gender. They stress on how women is the part of multiple oppressions and how these oppressions are impregnated in space and place. Fourth, the feminist geography asserts the importance of women as a subject of study and examines gender as a social and spatial process.[13]

Women in Geography: An Indian Perspective

The question of woman becomes important as she is often related to home; even her work is referred with reference to home (Relph, 1976; Tuan, 1971; Seamon, 1980). But, geography has always ignored the domestic; the home; the emotional or anything concerned with women till the very recent advent of feminist geography.[14] This resulted in the analysis of women's roles and changes in urban and regional structure and activity patterns[15]. The interesting part of this analysis was that geographers started seeing a relation between women and the place. They started studying and theorizing this relationship between process and spatial form on the basis of theory contextualized with women's lives to production and consumption.

Within the discipline many scholars started their work by criticizing the fact that women were either invisible within geographic literature or were analyzed as substitutes for men (Hayford, 1970; Burnett, 1973; Larimore, 1978; Tivers, 1978). And there emerged a '*geography of women*' which was concerned with socialist-feminist perspective on the relations between women and environment.[16] Another aspect which seeks attention is the insignificant number of women in the profession of academic geography in comparison to other social sciences. The studies done in this regard suggest that there is overwhelming male composition of human geography, especially in the past which is continuing to the present. [17] Feminists claim that this is one of the basic reasons why the discipline has primarily served the interests of men and worked within masculine paradigms. While some women did engage in exploring society, the knowledge created by them was not formally incorporated into the knowledge base of the discipline.[18] An example may be cited of Royal Geographic Society (RGS), where till 1915 women were not elected to membership in the RGS and fieldwork as geographic inquiry was limited to a few, elite, white males.[19]

Even in its demographic composition the discipline has been masculine in nature. A study by Lee (1990) shows that the women account for only 8 per cent as permanent academicians in various geography departments in the United States. As new doctorates and low ranking professors, women comprise a quarter of the faculty but only three percent of full professors, both in large and small departments. Although in 1990s in the United States, the women broke this barrier and entered graduate schools in large numbers. Women became part of the academic staff of many universities but were in junior positions.[20]

Women as Faculty

The situation is similar in the academics of Indian geography, where there appears to be resistance not only to the gender studies in geography but also to the entry of women in the academia.[21] This is mainly because the gender discourse is difficult to be placed in the traditional framework of Indian geography. And, over the period of time, women studies, as a distinct discipline outside geography, has developed as an academic statement of a political ideal of education.[22] Table 1 provides an insight on the scenario in the geography departments of eleven central universities of India in the year 2008-09. The table clearly shows that the gap between men and women professors is very large as there are only ten female professors compared to 41 male professors. The situation is worse in the slab of associate professors the number is three compared to 29 for men. The scenario seems to be friendlier now for women as the number of women assistant professors is more than compared to the other two designations (16 women and 26 men). Moreover, nearly one third of these universities (four out of eleven) employ only one woman. The adverse outcome of this deficit is that female students at the bachelor's, master's and doctoral level, lack role models of successful women as professional geographers.

Table 1 : Geographers in Academic Departments by Sex in some of the Central Universities of India (2008)

Central Universities with the Department of Geography	Professors		Associate Professors or Readers		Assistant Professors or Lecturers		Total number of Female Faculty Members in the Department*
	Males	*Females*	*Males*	*Females*	*Males*	*Females*	
Aligarh Muslim University (AMU), Aligarh	2	1	8	0	6	0	1 (17)
Benaras Hindu University (BHU). Varanasi	13	1	2	0	5	6	7 (27)
University of Allahabad, Allahabad	6	2	1	0	4	1	3 (14)
University of Delhi (DU), New Delhi	1	0	3	1	2	2	3 (9)
Jawaharlal Nehru University (JNU), New Delhi	7	2	6	1	2	3	6 (21)
Jamia Millia Islamia (JMI), New Delhi	5	2	2	1	3	3	6 (16)
Mizoram University, Imphal	1	0	1	0	1	0	0 (4)
North East Hill University (NEHU), Shillong	4	0	3	0	1	1	1 (9)
Manipur University, Imphal	2	0	1	0	2	0	0 (5)
University of Hyderabad, Hyderabad	0	1	0	0	0	0	1 (1)
Vishwabharati, Shantinekatan	0	1	2	0	0	0	1 (3)
Total	41	10	29	3	26	16	29 (126)

Note: The numbers in parenthesis denote the total number of faculty members in the Department of Geography. Only those universities have been taken on which information was available.

Source: Data has been analyzed from the information provided at the official websites of the concerned central universities

To get a better understanding of the scenario similar information was again collected in April 2017 from the websites of different Central and State universities were

Geography has been an established department. The state universities were included as with accordance to Government policy new central universities have come up were recruitment process is still in process. While in some state universities like that of Calcutta, Punjab, Bombay, Madras; the Department of Geography is quite old and has their own place in the overall development of the discipline. In total 45 such universities have been analyzed. The data in the table 2 gives a picture of women as faculty members in these universities either as assistant professors or associate professors or professors. It seems that women in Geography have frozen in time (West, 1995). In spite of considerable earlier optimism, there has been modest increase in the number of women faculty (from 23 per cent in 2008 to 31 per cent in 2017).

Another point of consideration is that the gap is largest among the professors. This indicates that there is gender discrimination within the discipline. Out of total 165 professors only 45 were women (27 per cent) which means that women faculty experiences greater rank disadvantage when it comes to larger educational institutions like universities. The greatest gains in the representation of women have been made at the stage of assistant professor (36 per cent), which gives an optimistic hope. But these data provide a scenario which depicts uneven progress of women in the discipline of geography as a profession. Though considerable gains have been made both in the absolute number and percentage of women faculty, they are still underrepresented. Why is this so? Without a detailed comparison of and length of time in departments it is difficult to attribute discrimination against women. One cannot judge who should own the responsibility; the so-called male biased promotion boards or lack of ambition on the part of women themselves. Many women academics have dual responsibilities on marriage; which somehow dents their climb on the academic ladder.

Table 2 : Geographers in Academic Departments by Sex in Some of the Central and State Universities of India (2017)

Central or State University	Professors		Associate Professor		Assistant Professor		Total		Total Faculty Members
	Male	Female	Male	Female	Male	Female	Male	Female	
Rajiv Gandhi University, Itanagar	3	2	1	0	1	1	5	**3**	8
Gauhati University, Gauhati	4	0	2	1	3	0	9	**3**	12
IGNOU, New Delhi	1	0	2	0	2	1	5	**1**	6
Jamia Millia Islamia, Delhi	5	3	0	0	0	3	5	**6**	11
JNU, New Delhi	7	4	2	1	2	3	11	**8**	19
Central University of Haryana, Mahendragarh	0	0	0	0	2	0	2	**0**	2
Central University of Karnataka, Gulbarga	1	0	0	1	0	2	1	**3**	4
The Indira Gandhi National Tribal University, Amarkantak	1	0	0	0	2	1	3	**1**	4
Manipur University, Imphal	1	0	1	0	2	1	4	**1**	5
North Eastern Hill University, Shilong	6	0	2	0	0	2	8	**2**	10
Mizoram University, Aizawal	3	0	1	0	4	0	7	**0**	7
Central University of Punjab, Bathinda	0	0	0	0	3	1	3	**1**	4
Sikkim University, Gangtok	0	0	1	0	5	0	6	**0**	6
Osmania University, Hyderabad	6	3	1	0	3	1	10	**4**	14
Tripura University, Agartala	0	0	0	1	1	3	1	**4**	5
Aligarh Muslim University, Aligarh	10	0	2	0	4	1	16	**1**	17
University of Allahabad, Allahabad	4	2	0	0	3	1	7	**3**	10
Banaras Hindu University, Varanasi	15	0	2	3	3	2	20	**5**	25

(Contd...)

H N B Garhwal University, Srinagar	7	0	3	2	2	0	12	**2**	14
Vishwa Bharati, Shantiniketan	4	2	1	0	0	1	5	**3**	8
University of Calcutta, Calcutta	3	1	2	1	4	0	9	**2**	11
Panjab University, Chandigarh	1	5			2	2	3	**7**	10
S P Pune University, Pune	2	1	1	1	3	2	6	**4**	10
University of Mumbai	1	1	0	2	4	2	5	**5**	10
Punjabi University, Patiala	2	1	0	0	1	3	3	**4**	7
Ranchi University, Ranchi	0	0	5	2	0	0	5	**2**	7
Rajasthan University	1	1	7	3	2	2	10	**6**	16
Jammu University	1	0	1	1	2	1	4	**2**	6
H P University,Shimla	1	0	1	0	1	1	3	**1**	4
Kurukshetra University	2	1	1	0	0	2	3	**3**	6
Gujarat University,Ahmedabad	0	0	0	0	2	0	2	**0**	2
Madras University, Chennai	2	0	0	0	3	0	5	**0**	5
Mysore University, Mysore	1	1	2	1	1	0	4	**2**	6
Ravenshaw University,Cuttack	1	0	0	2	3	1	4	**3**	7
University of North Bengal, Darjeeling	2	1	1	2	2	1	5	**4**	9
Mohan Lal Sukhadia University, Udaipur	4	2	0	0	0	0	4	**2**	6
Maharshi Dayanand University, Rohtak	8	2	1	1	0	0	9	**3**	12
Bangalore University, Bengaluru	2	0	0	0	0	0	2	**0**	2
Pt. Ravishankar Shukla University, Raipur	1	3	0	1	0	0	2	**3**	5
Utkal University, Bhubaneswar	1	0	2	0	1	1	4	**1**	5

(Contd...)

Maharaja Sayajirao University of Baroda	2	2	1	1	1	0	4	**3**	7
The University of Burdwan, Burdwan	2	2	1	0	3	2	6	**4**	10
Tilka Manjhi Bhagalpur University, Bhagalpur	2	0	0	1	0	0	3	**0**	3
Madurai Kamraj University, Madurai	0	0	1	0	2	1	3	**1**	4
Magadh University, Bodhgaya	4	1	0	0	0	0	4	**1**	5
Total	**124**	**41**	**48**	**28**	**79**	**45**	**252**	**114**	**366**

Source: Data has been analyzed from the information provided at the official websites of the concerned universities

Another interesting fact which shows that things have not yet changed for women is their representation in various geographical societies operating in India. The history of most of these societies, show gender discrimination at the highest level as hardly any women geographer has been at its top-most position of President or Director. Among the eight major societies (The Geographical Society of India; Indian National Cartographic Association; Deccan Geographical Society; Indian Institute of Geographers; Association of Punjab Geographers; The Indian Geographical society; The National Geographical Society of India; Rajasthan Geographical Society) only two had women as their Presidents in their entire history. INCA had Prof A. Banerjee as their President in 2015; while The Geographical Society of India had Prof P. K. Saha in 2013-14 and Prof. S. Ray from 2014 onwards. These statistics clearly portray that at pyramidal hierarchy males dominate the academic summit.

Women as Students

The above discussion clearly indicates that geography as a subject is dominated by a traditional male-orientated view of society and this becomes more apparent when one looks into the geography departments of various Indian universities, which are also heavily dominated by men. Another aspect which addresses this issue is the intake of female students at the Bachelor's, Master's and Diploma levels. Due to lack on information this analysis has been restricted only to the Department of Geography, Jamia Millia Islamia, New Delhi. This has been taken as a case study here, as it is located in the capital city of India. Moreover being a minority institute it attracts students from minority social and religious groups. Another significant reason for its selection is that this Department provides Geography in maximum number of under-graduate and post graduate courses. The data has been collected for last seven academic years to examine the proportion of female students at different levels.

Table 3: Proportion of Female Students at Different Levels of Study in the Department of Geography, Jamia Millia Islamia (2010-17)

Level of Study	2010-11		2011-12		2012-13		2015-16		2016-17	
	Male	Female	Male	Female	Male	Female	Male	Female	Male	Female
Bachelors (Honours)	33	18 (35.3 %)	40	17 (29.8%)	23	18 (43.9%)	41	26 (38.8%)	43	22 (33.8%)
Masters	16	12 (42.8%)	14	14 (50.0%)	14	12 (46.1%)	23	09 (28.1%)	26	09 (25.7%)
Ph.D	NA	NA	NA	NA	NA	NA	8	2 (20.0%)	10	2 (16.7%)
Diploma	15	8 (34.8%)	12	8 (40%)	15	8 (34.8%)	40	16 (28.6%)	14	12 (46.1%)
Certificate (Evening)	NA	NA	NA	NA	NA	NA	NA	NA	25	05 (16.7%)

Note: The numbers in parenthesis denote the proportion of female students to total students.

Source: Data has been analyzed from the information provided in the annual report of the Department for the respective years.

The data in table 3 again portrays the disadvantaged picture of female students. Surprisingly, the proportion of female students is better at the post graduate level. But this is not a happy situation as the proportion drastically decreases in research. This may be because of either lack of self-confidence or parental support to continue further studies. In addition, they have the example of a male-dominated academic profession (McDowell, 1979).

Moreover, they are fewer in number in professional courses in spite of the fact that they are of lesser duration.

To sum up, our discipline exemplifies the male ethos of Indian university life and how it discourages women. Both attitudes and behaviour are conditioned by the existing system and if we want to foster greater equality between both the sexes in both the profession as well as the academic study of geography we must act now before it's too late.

Perspectives for the future

The inclusion of women in the geographical analysis not only improves the investigations of geographical space but also become the pivot around which one can understand the gender inequalities. Thus, the *geography of women* has emerged as a key area in the discipline of geography which identifies gender relations and their variations in the local area and in future also, it will continue to produce diverse knowledge's and different interpretations within the broader perspective of feminism. Therefore, one working with geographies of women must come out of the dichotomies of home and work, formal and informal. Rather they should retain these dichotomies to provide a conceptual framework for their analysis on gender relations. The most common strategy should be to work from within existing ways of thinking about space and how it is being occupied. In other words, the geographers should break away from the notion of gender and sex as historically and geographically variable categories and should try to understand our bodies, our sex and our gender differently. This can be done by creating material and cultural spaces embodied with social constructions, attributes and ways of behaviour which construct one as men or women, masculine or feminine.

Secondly, as gender relations permeate all areas of social and economic life of man, a geographer analyzing space from this perspective should try to make gender relations and divisions part of analysis of social divisions, just as class and race have become. As by neglecting gender, we are overlooking a key element of the division of space and allocation of resources, thus, reducing the explanatory framework. Therefore, one should study the built environment in relation to gender as both are social constructions having a profound relationship. In other words, the challenge in front of the geographers is to include recognition and analysis of gender relations within geographical research. More so because the highly educated women are the primary latent labour force for the higher education in any region.

Conclusions

The above account clearly indicates that the *geography of women* significantly contributes to the deliberations in critical geography as well as feminist studies through its epistemological and methodological approaches. Some of the studies are oriented exclusively on women and their work, while others deal with gender relations and identities and how these have been transformed through their dynamic relations with the restructuring of work.[23] Secondly, it has brought the dichotomy of opposites – man and woman, nature and culture, public and private, production and reproduction – into the general theory and practice. As a result, a new discourse has emerged which focuses on the analyses of cultural representation; work on sexuality, subjectivity and social relations; and new developments in the studies of interrelationships of race, class and gender.[24] This discourse therefore presents challenges to female geographers and they have to make space within the existing frame avoiding any academic pitfalls. This can be done if the profession persists to pull women into geographical academia especially at the higher levels and remove glass ceiling. Furthermore, biases and prejudices which are gender based must be uncovered and eradicated. As Palm (1985) states that "by including more women in our field we will enjoy a significant infusion of new talent as well as the prospect of new perspectives on classic geographic problems".

References

- Bondi, L. and Davidson, J. 2005. Situating Gender in L. Nelson and J. Seager (ed.) *A Companion to Feminist Geography*. Blackwell Publishing House, London: pp. 15-31.
- Bowlby, S., Lewis, J., Mcdowell, L., and Foord, J. 1989. The Geography of Gender, in R. Peet and N. Thrift (ed.) *New Models in Geography: The Political Economy Perspective*, eds. Unwin Hyman, London.
- Breitbart, M. M. 1984. Feminist Perspectives in Geographic Theory and Methodology, *Antipode*, 6(3): 72-74.
- Dias, K. and Blecha, J. 2007. Feminism and Social Theory in Geography: An Introduction, *The Professional Geographer*, 59(1):1-9.
- Dyrc, I. 1993. Ethnography: A Feminist Method, *The Canadian Geographer*, 37(1):52-57.
- England, K. and V. Lawson, V. 2005. Feminist Analyses of Work: Rethinking the Boundaries, Gendering and Spatiality of Work, in L. Nelson and J. Seager (ed.) *A Companion to Feminist Geography*. Blackwell Publishing House, London: pp. 77-92
- Falconer Al-Hindi, K. 2000. Women in Geography in the 21st Century: Introductory Remarks: Structure, Agency and Women Geographers in Academia at the End of the Long Twentieth Century', *The Professional Geographer*, 52 (4): 697-702.
- Gregson, N. and et. al., 1997. Gender in Feminist Geography, in *Feminist Geographies: Explorations in Diversity and Difference*, ed. Women and Geography Study Group, Longman, London.
- Lee, D. R. 1990. The Status of Women in Geography: Things Change, Things remain the same, *The Professional Geographer*, 42(2): 202-211.
- Mackenzie, S., Foord, J and McDowell, L. 1980. Women's Place: Women's Space, Area, 12 (1): 47-51
- Mackenzie, S. 1984. Women and the Environment: Editorial Introduction, *Antipode*, 6 (3): 3-10.
- Mackenzie, S. 1989. Restructuring the relations of work and life:

women as environmental actors, feminism as geographic analysis, in A. Kobayashi and S. Mackenzie (ed.) *Remaking Human Geography* eds., Unwin Hyman, London: 40-59.

- McDowell, L. 1979. Women in British Geography, *Area*, 11(2): 151-154.
- Momsen, J. H. 1980. Women in Canadian Geography, *The Professional Geographer*, 32(3): 365-369.
- Monk, J. 2004. Women, Gender, and the Histories of American Geography, *Annals of the Association of American Geographers*, 94(1): 1–22.
- Moss, P. 1993. Focus: Feminism as Method, *The Canadian Geographer*, 37(1): 48-49.
- Nelson, L. and Seager, J. 2005. *A Companion to Feminist Geography*, Blackwell Publishing House, London.
- Peet, R. 1998. *Modern Geographical Thought*. Blackwell Publishers, Oxford.
- Poonacha, V. 2003. Women Studies in Indian Universities: Current Concerns, *Economic and Political Weekly*, June 23: 2653-58.
- Raju, S. 1991. Gender and Deprivation: A Theme Revisited with a Geographical Perspective, *Economic and Political Weekly*, 26 (49): 2827-2829.
- Raju, S. 2004. Gender and Geography in India: Why the Two shall Meet, in S. Banerjee Guha (ed.) *Space, Society and Geography*. Rawat Publications. New Delhi: pp.83-99.
- Rose, D. 1993. On Feminism, Method and Methods in Human Geography: An Idiosyncratic Overview, *The Canadian Geographer*. 37(1): 57-61.
- Rose, G. 1993. *Feminism and Geography: The Limits of Geographical Knowledge*. Polity Press, Cambridge.
- Rubin, B. 1979. Women in Geography Revisited: Present Status, New Options, *The Professional Geographer*, 11 (2): 125-134.
- Staeheli, L. A. and Martin, P. M., 2000. Places for Feminism in Geography, *Annals of the American Academy of Political and Social Science*, 571(September): 135-150.
- Townsend, J. G., 1991. Towards a Regional Geography of Gender, *The Geographical Journal*, 157(1): 25-35.
- Warf, B. 2006. *Encyclopedia of Human Geography*. Sage Publications, London.

- Winkler, J. A. 2000. Faculty Reappointment, Tenure, and Promotion: Barriers for Women, *The Professional Geographer*, 52(4): 737–750.

1 S. Mackenzie (1984) 'Women and the Environment: Editorial Introduction', *Antipode*, Vol.6, No. 3, p.3.

2 Falconer Al-Hindi, K. (2000) 'Women in Geography in the 21st Century: Introductory Remarks: Structure, Agency and Women Geographers in Academia at the End of the Long Twentieth Century', The Professional Geographer, Vol. 52, No. 4, November, p. 698.

3 R. Peet (1998) 'Feminist Theory and the Geography of Gender', in *Modern Geographical Thought*, Blackwell Publishers, Oxford, p.247.

4 L. Nelson and J. Seager (2005) 'A Companion to Feminist Geography', *Blackwell Publishing House*, London, p. 3.

5 L. Nelson and J. Seager (2005) 'A Companion to Feminist Geography', *Blackwell Publishing House*, London, p. 3.

6 S. Bowlby, J. Lewis, L. Mcdowell and J. Foord (1989) 'The Geography of Gender', in *New Models in Geography: The Political Economy Perspective*, (eds.) R. Peet and N. Thrift, Unwin Hyman, London, p. 157.

7 K. Dias and J. Blecha (2007) *Op. Cit. 4*, p. 2.

8 R. Peet (1998), *Op. Cit. 2*, p. 270.

9 S. Bowlby, J. Lewis, L. Mcdowell and J. Foord (1989) *Op. Cit. 5*, p. 158-59.

10 L. Bondi and J. Davidson (2005) 'Situating Gender' in *'A Companion to Feminist Geography'*, (eds.) L. Nelson and J. Seager, Blackwell Publishing House, London, p. 15.

11 Ibid, p. 16

12 L. Nelson and J. Seager (2005) *Op. Cit. 3*, p. 5.

13 Ibid, p. 6 - 7.

14 Ibid, p. 48

15 S. Mackenzie (1984), *Op. Cit. 3*, p. 3.

16 Ibid, p. 3

17 B. Warf (2006) 'Encyclopedia of Human Geography', *Sage Publications*, London, p. 157.

18 L. A. Staeheli and P. M. Martin (2000) 'Places for Feminism in Geography', *Annals of the American Academy of Political and Social Science*, Vol. 571, September, p. 138.

19 M. Damosh (1991) 'Toward a Feminist Historiography of Geography', Transactions to the Institute of British Geographers, Vol. 16, No. 1, p.97.

20 Ibid, p. 137

21 S. Raju (2004) 'Gender and Geography in India: Why the Two shall Meet', in *Space, Society and Geography* (ed.) S. Banerjee Guha, Rawat Publications, New Delhi, p. 84.

22 V. Poonacha (2003) 'Women Studies in Indian Universities: Current Concerns', *Economic and Political Weekly*, June 23, p. 2653.

23 K. England and V. Lawson (2005) 'Feminist Analyses of Work: Rethinking the Boundaries, Gendering and Spatiality of Work', in *'A Companion to Feminist Geography'*, (eds.) L. Nelson and J. Seager, Blackwell Publishing House, London, p. 87.

24 S. Bowlby, J. Lewis, L. Mcdowell and J. Foord (1989) *Op. Cit. 5*, p. 169.

References

- Berg, M. 2000. Women's Work, Mechanization and the Early Phases of Industrialisation in England, in P. Joyce (ed.) *The Historical Meanings of Work.* Cambridge University Press, New York.
- Bondi, L. and Davidson, J. 2005. Situating Gender in L. Nelson and J. Seager (ed.) *A Companion to Feminist Geography.* Blackwell Publishing House, London: pp. 15-31.
- Bowlby, S., Lewis, J., Mcdowell, L., and Foord, J. 1989. The Geography of Gender, in R. Peet and N. Thrift (ed.) *New Models in Geography: The Political Economy Perspective,* eds. Unwin Hyman, London.
- Breitbart, M. M. 1984. Feminist Perspectives in Geographic Theory and Methodology, *Antipode,* 6(3): 72-74.
- Bullock, S. 1994. *Women and Work.* Zed Books, London.
- Dias, K. and Blecha, J. 2007. Feminism and Social Theory in Geography: An Introduction, *The Professional Geographer,* 59(1):1-9.
- Dyrc, I. 1993. Ethnography: A Feminist Method, *The Canadian Geographer,* 37(1):52-57.
- England, K. and V. Lawson, V. 2005. Feminist Analyses of Work: Rethinking the Boundaries, Gendering and Spatiality of Work, in L. Nelson and J. Seager (ed.) *A Companion to Feminist Geography.* Blackwell Publishing House, London: pp. 77-92

- Gregson, N. and et. al., 1997. Gender in Feminist Geography, in *Feminist Geographies: Explorations in Diversity and Difference*, ed. Women and Geography Study Group, Longman, London.
- Harding, S. and Norberg, K. 2005. New Feminist Approaches to Social Science Methodologies: An Introduction, *Signs: Journal of Women in Culture and Society*, 30(4)
- Mackenzie, S. 1984. Women and the Environment: Editorial Introduction, *Antipode*, 6(3): 3-10.
- Mackenzie, S. 1989. Restructuring the relations of work and life: women as environmental actors, feminism as geographic analysis, in A. Kobayashi and S. Mackenzie (ed.) *Remaking Human Geography* eds., Unwin Hyman, London: 40-59.
- Moss, P. 1993. Focus: Feminism as Method, *The Canadian Geographer*, 37(1): 48-49.
- Nelson, L. and Seager, J. 2005. *A Companion to Feminist Geography*, Blackwell Publishing House, London.
- O'Brien, R. and Williams, M. 2004. *Global Political Economy: Evolution and Dynamics*, Pal grave, Macmillan.
- Oberhauser, A. M., 2000. Feminism and Economic Geography: Gendering Work and Working Gender in E. Sheppard and T. J. Barnes (ed.) *A Companion to Economic Geography*, Blackwell Publishers, Oxford, pp. 60-76.
- Pahl, R. E. 1992. Defining Work in L. Mcdowell and R. Pringle (ed.) *Defining Women: Social Institutions and Gender Divisions*, Polity Press, Cambridge.
- Parikh, J. and Garg, P. K. 1989. *Indian Women: An Inner Dialogue*. Sage Publications, New Delhi.
- Peet, R. 1998. *Modern Geographical Thought*. Blackwell Publishers, Oxford.
- Poonacha, V. 2003. Women Studies in Indian Universities: Current Concerns, *Economic and Political Weekly*, June 23: 2653-58.
- Raju, S. 2004. Gender and Geography in India: Why the Two shall Meet, in S. Banerjee Guha (ed.) *Space, Society and Geography*. Rawat Publications. New Delhi: pp.83-99.
- Rao, S. 1999. Women-as-symbol: The intersections of Identity Politics, Gender and Indian Nationalism, *Women's International Forum*, 22(3): 317-328.
- Rose, D. 1993. On Feminism, Method and Methods in Human

Geography: An Idiosyncratic Overview, *The Canadian Geographer.* 37(1): 57-61.

- Rose, G. 1993. *Feminism and Geography: The Limits of Geographical Knowledge*. Polity Press, Cambridge.
- Shah, K. K., 2005. *History and Gender: Some Explorations*, Rawat Publications, New Delhi.
- Staeheli, L. A. and Martin, P. M., 2000. Places for Feminism in Geography, *Annals of the American Academy of Political and Social Science*, 571(September): 135-150.
- Townsend, J. G., 1991. Towards a Regional Geography of Gender, *The Geographical Journal*, 157(1): 25-35.
- Warf, B. 2006. *Encyclopedia of Human Geography*. Sage Publications, London.

2

Migration and Women

Arundhati Bhattacharyya

Introduction

Today, around 3.3 per cent of the human population are living outside their country of birth, i.e., they have migrated. Migration may not be a one-way event, taking place. It can be a loop with movements taking place in a circular movement or going back and forth. (Matias Echanove, Rahul Srivastava, 2017) Migration is a complex phenomenon, where variety of matters is associated with it. Migration can create greater opportunities for few, who are more skilled than others. The employers in the distant land may attract such migration. An individual may be migrating several times in one's life or it can be that s/he may be migrating only once in a lifetime. Floating migrants may have an important role in running the economy. Traditionally, the economic aspect of migration was more focussed on by the researchers in the field. Slowly, other aspects of migration, like, its impact on the incumbent and his/her life, cultural and social aspects of migration, the link between the country of origin and migration and its impact on the migrant and his/her family etc, became the areas of study. Usually, a migrant from an under-developed country moves to a developing country. They, generally, do not migrate directly to developed nations. Statistics state that only 1 per cent of the migrants from Africa move over to Europe. (Lansink, 2009) Migration creates myriads of maladies.

Migration may be voluntary or forced. With the rise of increasing tensions and disturbances, throughout the world, the level of forced migration has also increased. This has social, political, economic, cultural repercussions. In case of forced migration, the push factor becomes the determining one. The forcibly displaced refugee or internally displaced people run away from their place of origin due to life threatening situations, which may include disease, riots, armed conflict, discrimination, persecution, terrorism, wars, tribal skirmishes, insurgencies etc. Poverty is another major reason pushing migrants to leave their place of origin. Gross unemployment can also be a reason for migration. A migrant can have their unique reason to move over to destinations, unknown in multifarious aspects. But, it is a tough decision, which requires lot of courage. All migrations do not end in good life of the incumbent. The event of migration may turn to be trauma of a lifetime. The Asian migration scene is seeing a new form of cross-border sex terrorism. The positive aspect is that some non government organisations, like, the Self Empowerment Programme of Migrant Women (SEPOM) in Thailand are doing good job in trying to improve the condition of the condition of the migrant workers in Thailand who return after having horrible experience in Japan. Their work is turning to be commendable. (Bose, 2003)

Migration and Its Impact on Women

Among the migrant domestic workers, 11.5 million are international migrants. About 8.5 million of the migrant domestic workers are women. Female migrants can contribute to the economy of the country. There have been studies which have revealed that women migrants remit more of their income back home, compared to male migrants. (Martin, 2003) For example, in 1999, in Sri Lanka, 62 per cent of the remittances came from female migrants. (Karwar)

In the 1960s and the early 1970s, the migrant was usually the male. The invisibility of the women migrants was there. Female migration has been a neglected area. (Zai Liang and Yiu Por Chen, 2004) In the 1970s and the 1980s, researches on migration had started to include women. Today, gender is an integral part of the migration process. (Monica Boyd, Elizabeth Grieco, 2003) In the period of 1971-2001, the growth rate of female migration was 2.24 per cent, while that of the male was 1.85 per cent. (Arpita Banerjee, Saraswati Raju, 2009) In 2015, around 244 million people have migrated from the country of origin. Almost half of the migrants are women. Migration may be a matter of choice, rather than that of compulsion. There are push and pull factors leading to migration. Among the reasons behind migration of women, marriage has been the main factor. Associational migration for female population has always been high. A study by Marsden and Tepperman in Canada in the 1980s, reveal that the migrant women, especially, migrant wives are the greatest sufferers and losers. Here, the occupational benefits of the husband are taken into granted when the couple migrate. The wives may miss the social interactions, networking, or the job she has left behind, in order to adjust to the need of migration for the husband's occupational mobility. The rise in unemployment in different parts of the world may make the search for employment for the migrant wife more difficult. In various stages of her life, unknowingly, she may be sucked into the category of unpaid work. In this study, it was found that there was men-led pattern for migration, which destined women to migrate. (Lorna R. Marsden, Lorne J. Tepperman, 1985) Many a times, her wishes are trampled in order to fit into the demands of society.

Women are often looked at as non-subjects. They may enjoy some form of secondary citizenship. The patriarchal State have, at times, provided step motherly treatment to women migrants. (Manchanda, 2004) Traditionally, the identity and citizenship of a woman was totally dependent on the father or the husband. Even today, citizenship rules in many countries provide prerogative to the father than to the mother regarding determination of the child's citizenship. So, in these countries, the father has greater legal rights than the mother in deciding the destiny of the child. A single mother with a child faces greater harassment in the process of migration in many countries.

Forced migrations are taking place today in the world. Such migrations may be due to man-made or natural causal factors. The women and the children are the worst sufferers, in such process of forced migration. Evidences are found among Rohingya refugees, Chakma refugees, Tamil refugees, refugees from Syria, Afghanistan and those who are forced to leave their own country. If a woman enters foreign destination as an undocumented migrant, she is more prone to get trafficked and exploited. Her identity gets trampled as she is only a 'victim'. The dislocation in their lives disempowers them to the hilt. They may fall prey to all sorts of trafficking taking place in the difficult process of migration. These refugees who are forced to migrate reach a foreign land where she does not know the language, culture, norms etc. She is an 'outsider' there. She is not aware of the legal and political rights which are available to her and her children under the international humanitarian laws. The traffickers may have their targets in the refugee camps, where the migrants, including women and children are taking refuge. The marginalisation faced by the vulnerable is severe and so are the forms of exploitation.

The rise of demand of women labour, in the form of domestic help, ayah, caretaker, nurse etc. has become the basis for the rise of the pull factor in migration. (Arpita Banerjee, Saraswati Raju, 2009) This has led to poor or lower middle class women migrate to urban areas or abroad, in search of better pay and facilities. This helps the woman to improve the condition of her family back home. Instances have been found in South India; where a woman has gone abroad in order to help her family to come out of the debt-ridden condition. Many work as domestic workers abroad. They send their remittance back home. In the Gulf, some of the women domestic workers live in social and psychological isolation. (Shah, 2004) Tables 1 and 2 provide a picture of the position of the migrant domestic workers and the women migrant domestic workers, respectively. Table 1 represents that the Arab States have the highest migrant domestic workers, while North America has the lowest migrant domestic workers. Table 2 represents that the Arab States have the highest women migrant domestic workers, while East Europe has the lowest migrant women domestic workers.

There is need to improve their condition. The Government of India, by exception, has come to their help when they have faced problem. But there is need of organised policy making and tight implementation through diplomacy by governments of all the countries.

Table 1: Migrant Domestic Workers (%)

AREAS	(%)
ARAB STATES	27
SE ASIA AND THE PACIFIC	19
NORTH, SOUTH & WEST EUROPE	19
EAST ASIA	10
LATIN AMERICA & THE CARIBBEAN	7
NORTH AMERICA	6

Source: 'Migrant Domestic Workers', *The Economic Times*, 25 November, 20 16, p 16

Table 2: Women Migrant Domestic Workers (%)

AREAS	(%)
ARAB STATES	61
SE ASIA AND THE PACIFIC	39
NORTH, SOUTH & WEST EUROPE	11
EAST ASIA	34
LATIN AMERICA & THE CARIBBEAN	36
NORTH AMERICA	3
SUB-SAHARAN AFRICA	9
SOUTH ASIA	3
CENTRAL & WEST ASIA	5
EAST EUROPE	1
NORTH AFRICA	23

Source: 'Migrant Domestic Workers', *The Economic Times,* 25 November, 2016, p 16

Across the globe, women are engaged in the domestic services. In many places, they are not considered as economic activities. So, the remuneration and the other facilities one is supposed to get are absent. They may be considered to be beyond the borders of the remunerative labour market. The breadwinner is the man and the woman is always the 'dependent'. So, she, at times, is ready to compromise as the inferior worker. She may become the victim of the unwitting process of the exclusion rendered by the market system.

The care givers from the migrant population can become an intrinsic part of the economy of the country of destination. The global South is contributing to the migration process. Under-development in the global South, the emergence of neo-liberal economic policies, growth of economic integration, restructuring of the structural aspects, withdrawal of the State from welfare norms, increasing role of the World Bank and the International Monetary Fund in deciding the fate of the developing world etc may augment the rise in the movement of care workers throughout the world. Globalization has augmented migration process. Care-givers can be considered as emotional labourers. They need to love and care for the children, elderly, specially-abled population, just like they would care for their own family. They need to have empathy, while performing their activities. The relationship between the care-giver and their employers' family plays a significant role in the performance and quality of the job. Employing a domestic worker can address to the improvement of the status of the middle class families. Skill upgradation of the migrant domestic worker is being given importance. Though in very few countries where there are qualifications required to be a care-giver for the infants and the elderly. Training is slowly being imparted. This is a way of socialisation and internalisation of the norms of the destination country, so that they take care of the 'new' families in a professional manner and not continue to behave in their indigenous ways. Vocational training may be available for some. (Scrinzi, 2011) The care-givers may suffer from poor physical health, injury, fatigue, stress, depression, isolation etc which may also lead to death. They are hardly covered under health insurance. (Eckenwiler, 2011) This is the economic aspect of the wider social exclusion process. This is another part of the disparity that the society is witnessing against women and countless incidents of discriminatory process that goes on, almost invisibly. Her irregular status creates insecurities, which are well exploited by the agents. The domestic worker may fail to protest the discrimination and exploitation faced by her, as, in many circumstances, she has huge debts back home. She does not have any alternative as whatever she gets is essential for her. Her work relation may turn to be an extension of the patriarchal relations. (Morokvasic, 1984) Family control continues to determine her life chances. A study of transnational migrant women regarding Filipina domestic workers state that when migration takes place, in many cases, they lose social status and class. (Eycka, 2007) It can be possible that once a woman migrates to an unknown destination, her bargaining power reduce. Social insecurities can also affect her work and life, after migration.

On the other hand, there have been studies in the United States, like that of Patricia R. Pessar, where it was found that women gain in independence and autonomy once they migrate. Their ability to acquire economic opportunities may rise. Optimism about the opportunities of life may rise among women once they acquire higher levels of freedom. (Zai Liang and Yiu Por Chen, 2004) The limitations of culture and norms back home may fade away in the new location base, where she can start a new way of living, which was unknown to her, earlier. There is selective assimilation. Here, the migrants select the components of the culture of the destination country, which they would like to adopt. (Emilio A. Parrado, Chenoa A. Flippen, 2005) The constraints of the traditional gender hierarchies may be overcome by deliberate efforts. New role models and success stories can motivate the migrant women to achieve greater heights. As she may take new employment opportunities in the new location, she may start to have control over the budget and other forms of decision making. Their bargaining power increases. She may have greater voice regarding control of her own life and that of her children. They may start protesting against domestic violence, which they had not done before. They can also ask their husbands to participate in the household chores, in their own ways. The male hegemony as practised in the traditional societies may be contested by the migrant wives, as the destination country may have strict laws of equality. The liberal Western values may slowly get internalised by the migrant families. There may be more and more parity in the division of labour. (Emilio A. Parrado, Chenoa A. Flippen, 2005)

Diificulties in the Path of Migrant Women and the Ways to Improve Their Position

Migrant women may face violations of the right to free movement, right to speech and expression, right to equality, right to privacy, right to remuneration, right to equality, right to form association, right to food, right to safe and healthy workplace, with a harassment-free environment, right to dignified living etc.

Care giving by migrant women is a difficult job, as there are no time limits. The demands on them are also high. Violation of human rights of migrant women, in its myriad forms, does take place. Few countries are ready to accept migrants in their public space. The States may not favour multi-culturalism. Migrants face racism and ghettoisation. (Manuela Coppola, Lidia Curti, Laura Fantone, Marie-Hélène Laforest, Susanna Poole, 2004)

The United Nations and the International Labour Organisation have always come forward to improve the quality of life of migrant women. (Martin, 2003) The International Covenant on Civil and Political Rights (1966), the International Covenant on Economic, Social and Cultural Rights (1966), and the Convention on the Elimination of All Forms of Discrimination Against Women (1979) all support rights of the migrants. The United Nations Convention on the Protection of the Rights of all Migrant Workers and their Families (CMW) (1990) is a comprehensive document providing rights to the migrants. (Lansink, 2009) This was adopted by the General Assembly of the United Nations. The treaty is quite detailed in nature. Ratification of the treaty has been a difficult proposition for the migrant receiving countries. Protection of the human rights of the migrant population needs to be protected. The needs of the protection of the migrant should not change with the class, caste, gender, race etc of the migrant. The rights of the migrants should be universal in nature. A human being is entitled to basic rights. No country has the right to violate these rights. On 1st July 2003, the International Convention on the Protection of the Rights of All Migrant Workers and Members of Their Families (Migrant Workers' Convention) came into force. This was a revolutionary step taken in order to protect the rights of the migrant workers. It was a result of building consensus over a long time. (Satterthwaite, 2004) Conventions of the International Labour Organisation have provided labour rights to migrants. Some of them are Forced Labour Convention, 1930 (No. 29), Freedom of Association Convention, 1948 (87), Equal Remuneration Convention, 1951 (No. 100), Abolition of Forced Labour Convention, 1957 (No 105), Right to Organise and Collective Bargaining Convention, 1949 (105) etc. Migrant women are highly engaged to domestic work. But, there are only 22 countries that have ratified the International Labour Organisation Convention of Domestic Workers (189). It recognized the difficulties and the vulnerabilities faced by the women domestic workers. The migrant women would be highly benefitted by ratification of this Convention by more and more countries. (Gabaccia, 2017) Though there are several other legal arrangements, but, there are gaps existing between theory and practice. Lack of political does prevent countries to implement these Conventions.

Today, the developed countries are creating strict restrictions on migrants. The Governments of the world need to formulate policies regarding treatment of migrants. Proper ratification and implementation of the international conventions are equally important. The protection of the human rights of the migrants is the need of the hour.

Conclusion

There is need to put in place a well informed policy regarding forced migration anywhere in the world. If the country is governed by features of good governance, like, accountability, transparency, rule of law, protection of human rights etc, an individual will be happy to remain in one's country of origin. Moreover, if proper source of employment is there, then, the incumbent will not be attracted to the 'push' or the 'pull' factors. (Migration, 2015) There is need of restricting the 'push' factors, so that none are forced to migrate in search of better living. (Bose, 2003)

The States need to have the political will to protect the rights of the migrant workers, including that of the women. (Lansink, 2009) In spite of the invisible and visible discriminations from the host countries, women migrants should try to engage in networking and socialisation among themselves, so that they can share their joys and sorrows. The nongovernmental organisations and the civil society can support them. Migration has been taking place, since time immemorial. However, there is need to protect the rights of the migrants in all countries, in every situation to have a peaceful and egalitarian global society.

References

Manuela Coppola, Lidia Curti, Laura Fantone, Marie-Hélène Laforest, Susanna Poole. (2004). Women, Migration and Precarity. *Feminist Review, No. 87, Italian Feminisms* , 94-103.

Arpita Banerjee, Saraswati Raju. (2009). Gendered Mobility: Women Migrants and Work in Urban India. *Economic and Political Weekly* , 115-123.

Bose, A. (2003). Migrant Women Workers: Victims of Cross-Border Sex 'Terrorism' in Asia . *Economic and Political Weekly* , 868-869.

Eckenwiler, L. (2011). Women on the move: Long-term care, migrant women, and global justice . *International Journal of Feminist Approaches to Bioethics* , 1-31.

Emilio A. Parrado, Chenoa A. Flippen. (2005). Migration and Gender among Mexican Women. *American Sociological Review* , 606-632.

Eycka, K. V. (2007, April). *Women and Migration in Asia: Migrant Women and Work, Volume 4 by Anuja Agrawal*. Retrieved April 28, 2017, from http://www.jstor.org/stable/25548214

Gabaccia, D. (2017, January 16). *Take five: Migration and women's rights — where do we go from here?* . Retrieved May 9, 2017, from United Nations Women: http://www.unwomen.org/en/news/stories/2017/1/take-five-donna-gabaccia

Karwar, M. (n.d.). Gender and Migration: Why are Women More Vulnerable?

Lansink, A. (2009). Migration and development: The contribution of women migrant workers to poverty alleviation . *Agenda: Empowering Women for Gender Equity, No. 81, GENDER & POVERTY REDUCTION* , 126-136.

Lorna R. Marsden, Lorne J. Tepperman. (1985). The Migrant Wife: The Worst of All Worlds. *Journal of Business Ethics* , 205-213.

Manchanda, R. (2004). Gender Conflict and Displacement: Contesting 'Infantilisation' of Forced Migrant Women . *Economic and Political Weekly* , 4179-4186 .

Martin, S. F. (2003). *Women and Migration: Background Paper for the Consultative Meeting on Migration, Mobility and How this Movement affects Women.* United Nations Division for the Advamcement of Women.

Matias Echanove, Rahul Srivastava. (2017, March 12). Our Lives are 50-50. *The Hindu* , p. 6.

Migration. (2015, December 23). Retrieved April 26, 2017, from United Nations Population Fund: http://www.unfpa.org/migration

Monica Boyd, Elizabeth Grieco. (2003, March 1). *Women and Migration: Incorporating Gender into International Migration Theory.* Retrieved April 24, 2017, from Migration Policy Institute: http://www.migrationpolicy.org/article/women-and-migration-incorporating-gender-international-migration-theory

Morokvasic, M. (1984). Birds of Passage are also Women... . *The International Migration Review: Special Issue: Women in Migration* , 886-907.

Satterthwaite, M. (2004). Women Migrants' Rights under International Human Rights Law. *Feminist Review, No. 77, Labour Migrations: Women on the Move* , 167-171.

Scrinzi, F. (2011). Gender, migration and the ambiguous enterprise of professionalizing domestic service: the case of vocational training for the unemployed in France. *Feminist Review* , 153-172.

Shah, N. M. (2004). Gender and Labour Migration to the Gulf Countries . *Feminist Review, No. 77, Labour Migrations: Women on the Move* , 183-185.

Zai Liang and Yiu Por Chen. (2004). Migration and Gender in China: An Origin Destination Linked Approach . *Economic Development and Cultural Change* , 423-443.

3

Working Women in India: The Need for a Paradigm Shift in Gender Role Perceptions in Society and Workplaces

Nirupama Patwardhan and Shubhasheesh Bhattacharya

Introduction

For over four decades there has been increasing debate and concern regarding problems and challenges in the work-family domain. This interest has occurred on account of issues such as the influx of growing numbers of women into the workforce and changing definitions of 'work' itself which is further fuelled by rapid changes in technology, mechanization, modernization of production processes, high growth of the service industry etc

Just as definitions of 'work' and what it constitutes are changing, so are definitions of what constitutes 'family'. Consequently definitions of gender roles are also changing, to cater to these new definitions a new perspective is imperative, India cannot ignore the changes in the societal order and still hope to progress.

From an academic and societal perspective in many developed nations Work and family and gender studies have developed into a distinct area of research in their own right. In North America and Europe there are organisations that have been specifically set up to study shifting demographics and its impact on work and family as well as the wellbeing of individuals

As the Indian economy is being touted as one that may become the next superpower it is a crying shame that in academia as well as the society Indian research displays a distinct shortfall in gender, work and family studies. One of the reasons for this is a gender insensitive culture which accords a low standing to women and consequently women's issues. Studies related to gender specific work issues and their impact on the economy are even more critical, the contribution of women to the 'Nation Building' process cannot be ignored anymore if India is to develop into an academically strong and socially forward looking country.

The Global Workforce

The world over, countries are grappling with major shortages of qualified human resources. Shifts in demography, societal development, poor educational programmes, influences of globalisation, outsourcing etc are effecting not just general talent availability but also specific competencies and skill sets that are essential in emerging economies like India. Experts predict that this situation will develop into a more acute and extensive trend spanning across more skill sets and types of jobs over the next decade.

In 1987 The Hudson Institute published Workforce 2000 by W. B. Johnston, which was a graphic narrative of probable changes in the workforce and the world of work. Today 30 years later many of these predictions have actually materialized. As forecasted by the author, organisations are dealing with a different workforce in the new millennium, far diverse from the 'male dominated' one of the past which they were used to managing.

The new '*GLOBAL*' workforce is more culturally diverse with more women, working mothers, dual-earner families, single parents, employees with eldercare responsibilities and those from the sandwich generation (i.e. people with responsibilities of both children and elderly).

Gender, Gender Roles and Stereotypes

Gender implies the concept of maleness or femaleness. It is characterised by physical characteristics, psychological and behavioral tendencies, abilities, behaviour patterns, self image traits and is primarily used to differentiate between men and women.

Gender roles are the outlook that society, groups and individuals carry regarding what is typically expected from a person of a specific gender. These gender roles have come into being through individual's interactions with the environment which has led to certain beliefs about what type of behaviour is appropriate and should be exhibited by a particular gender. (Eagly and Steffen, 1984).

Stereotypes are defined as 'an oversimplified standardised image of a person or group'. Stereotypes subsist in all cultures and societies and are based on generally built beliefs, practices and norms, in most cases stereotypical beliefs are rigid but can be broken down given enough time. (Eagly and Steffen, 1984).

According to The United Nations Human Rights Commission stereotypes are not always negative but because they do not take into consideration many factors and can show a high level of prejudice. Negative stereotypes especially linked to gender, limit opportunity and choice and therefore are one of the root causes of gender discrimination; this ensures that women are deprived of sometimes even certain fundamental rights, freedom and privileges.

General viewpoints regarding how men and women are or ought to be make up the backbone of gender stereotypes.

The essence of stereotypes has been researched expansively and studies have been able to identify what typical attributes differentiate men and women (Diekman & Eagly, 2000; Abele, 2003)

Characteristic examples of how stereotypes shape the perception of gender roles and consequently translate into behavioural outcomes can be seen in everyday life; in the society it can be seen through acts such as honour killings, domestic violence, forced marriage and worse practices and in the workplace issues such as work-related segregation, unequal pay gaps, the glass ceiling effect, not being promoted to higher positions, fewer recommendations for rewards and impediments to career advancement are some of the overt problems women face because of it (Brett & Stroh, 1997: Rudman, 1998; Heilman & Chen, 2005)

Heilman, (1983, 2001) and Eagly & Karau, (2002); state that there is a perception about women being a ' poor fit' for certain work roles which have been traditionally considered a male bastion and hence the belief is that women not having the attributes supposedly necessary for such roles would fail or not succeed in these male 'gender-typed' positions. In such situations these gender stereotypes also encourage bias and create 'negative performance expectations' which compounds the problem.

Biases also lead to the creation of some approved standards of behaviour termed as "shoulds" and "should not's" that when defied women tend to face censure and social rejection, especially when they attain a certain level of success in their occupations (Heilman, 2001; Heilman et al., 2004: Heilman & Okimoto, 2007).

In India traditionally women were always perceived from an economic perspective as a financial drain because it was a surety that they would leave the parental house along with a hefty 'dowry' and consequently their priorities and loyalty would shift to their marital home and husband (Varma 2002; Singh 2002). Therefore it has been noted that

Indian parents tend to expect very little from their daughters in terms of emotional or financial support (Singh 2002). The role and status of women in India thus is dependent on her role as a wife or mother and principally is active only in the limits of her home. Even today even if women work outside the home they are still held answerable for domestic chores, childcare and eldercare.

The Public versus Private Sphere Model

The public versus private sphere model is based on the concept of "gendered categories" this is defined as 'approved roles for men and women' this work has highlighted a separation of a public or male sphere and a private or female sphere. Anderson (1988) and Peterson and Runyan (1999) built on this model. Table 1 presents a summary of the traits that define each sphere.

Table 1: Gender differences associated with the Public and Private Spheres

Factor	Masculine Role Associations (Public Sphere)	Feminine Role Associations (Private sphere)
Approved role and work	Production of goods and services	Domestic duties, childbearing etc.
Type of work	Paid labour	Unpaid labour
Perception at work	Leaders	Followers
Role type	Primary/Superior	Secondary/Inferior
Visibility in society	Visible	Invisible

Source: Adapted from Anderson (1988) and Peterson and Runyan (1999).

From this model it can be seen that traditionally, women and their work is linked to the domestic sphere. This type of work is invisible and is a part of the private sphere and hence not recognised by society. Further understanding of the table highlights the supposition that woman are 'followers' – this is an important finding from the viewpoint of the work sphere and would account for the reason why many times women are put in jobs that are beneath their abilities and skills on the assumption that they would always prioritise their domestic and/or reproductive roles ahead of that of a leadership role in the workplace. Anderson (1988) further goes on to say that the private sphere is viewed as inferior since it is associated with women, whereas the public sphere is identified as positive being linked to men.

The Indian Perspective: Equality Delusion

For many years the sex ratio in India has been skewed against women. In 2014 India's population was an estimated 1.26 billion; the last Census Survey of India (2011) indicates that for every 1,000 men there are only 940 women, which means that the female population stands at about 47 per cent of the total population.

Another disturbing fact is that India's female labour force participation (FLFP) rate is one of the lowest in the world even among emerging markets and developing countries and is about 28 percent as of 2016 figures. (Catalyst, 2017). This rate is well below the global average of about 50 percent and even more below the East Asia average of 63 percent. (World Bank report, 2017)

India's ranking on the gender inequality index is 127 and on the global gender gap index, it is 108, which is not astonishing when the latest government statistics are considered. For example if the FLFP rate stands at 33 percent this means that of the 380 million eligible to work women 125 million only are either working or are seeking employment. (Census of India 2011). Moreover, since 2004-05 in contrast to most other regions it has been found that FLFP in India is showing a declining trend and stands at 22.5 percent in 2011-2012 down from 29.4 percent in 2004-2005. (ILO)

Furthermore, amongst the G-20 economies India's gender gap in participation standing at 50 percent is one of the widest. (World Bank report, 2017). The gender gap in the labour force is seen to be predominantly severe in the 15-59 age groups where for women in rural areas the participation is only 32 percent compared to 83 percent for men and in urban areas 21 percent compared to 81 percent for men (Census of India, 2011). According to the ILO, in 2011-12, whilst 62.8 percent of women were engaged in the agriculture sector, only 20 percent were working in industry and 17 percent in varied service sectors.

Working Women and the Impact on the Economy; the Benefits of Inclusivity

It is a curious fact that even in the so called liberated and democratic 'West' the figures for women in terms of acceptance, visibility and contribution at higher levels of business, administration and management are surprisingly low. In the book 'The Equality Illusion, The Truth about Women and Men Today', the author, Kat Banyard states that women constitute only 11 per cent of the top executives and four per cent of CEOs and heads of boards in the fifty largest publicly traded corporations in the European Union. Even in the United States women hold about 16.9 percent of Fortune 500 board seats, 14.6 percent of executive positions and of the top earners they make up approximately 8.1 percent (Centre for American Progress Fact sheet 2014)

In India very limited research has been conducted on women's representation in management the few statistics that are available however that when it comes to managerial jobs women lag far behind men. Kulkarni (2000), Chadha (2002), Mehra (2002) and Singh (2003) report that women's participation rates range from as low as around 3 percent of all administrative positions to approximately a high of 5.8 percent. Additionally Koshal, et al (2006), state that only 2 women take administrative and managerial positions for every 100 men.

In 2009 The Confederation of Indian Industry released a study "Understanding the Levels of Empowerment of

Women in the Workplace in India" the study reports that in the 149 medium and large size companies that were surveyed across regions in India, there were 16 percent women at junior management level, 4 percent each at middle and senior levels, and only 1 percent in organizational leadership positions (CEOs).

A study conducted by the research agency Catalyst showed that organisations that had more women officers posted higher return on equity sometimes as high as. 35.1 percent. This is a forceful argument for organisations in India to go the extra mile to retain women employees, specifically at higher levels of management.

However if more women are to work and maybe ultimately reach the top of their respective organisations a clear understanding and shift in the way the various 'roles' of women are perceived needs to be debated in corporate and academic circles and even more importantly the society in general.

Gender disparity in the workplace and at home has a harmful impact on women. Furthermore research shows that this issue considerably affects how the economy and ultimately the country grows. A report by McKinsey in 2015, states that by just narrowing the gender gap within the labour force, India would be able to increase the GDP by approximately 2.9 trillion annually by the year 2050.

Challenges for Working Women in India

Notwithstanding the fact that education enrollment rates and female literacy has been on the rise over the last few decades, India still has poor levels of women's workforce participation. (Indian Census 2011)

There remains a vast gender gap in terms of number of women employed in the labour force as well as in the 'kind' of work women perform. While India remains largely an agrarian economy, it is consequently observed that a significant section of India's working women are occupied in agricultural activities. Economists and experts argue that with a budding economy, industrial development and proliferation of urbanization, more and more women ought to be entering the labor force specifically into other prolific sectors such as the service sector or manufacturing, but unfortunately this has not been the case.

1. Basic cultural and social issues

While the last few decades has definitely witnessed a change in parental attitude towards girls, and parents are ever more agreeable to spending on the education of their daughters in both rural and urban India, the thought of a woman functioning outside the home is still culturally difficult to accept for many. Added to this is the concept of "family honor," and the well-established concepts of 'the correct gender role' for a female. There is also an unnatural fear of the social implications of a woman being economically empowered which prevents many from allowing even highly educated daughters to work outside the house.

The heinous gang rape in 2014 of a student in New Delhi has flamed ever-growing concerns about the safety of women, increasing reports in the media from other parts of the country of sexual assaults and violence against working women in cities, has fuelled public perception that women who step out of the house for work are at a huge risk and this further solidifies these unfair gender stereotypes and act as deterrents to women seeking meaningful employment outside the home.

In rural as well as urban settings if women are in some way able to break the bonds of such societal limitations many find it difficult to get stable and better paying jobs, for many they end up in clerical, menial or informal, semi- or unskilled sectors, where pay is limited and most other job benefits non-existent.

Despite more women entering the formal labour market, there has been very slight or no change in the pattern of domestic responsibilities. Studies reveal that women still continue to take on the lion's share of household chores, and child care responsibilities. (Singh 2004). At the same time studies have found that many employers fall short in providing sufficient maternity and childcare support to working mothers, leaving them crippled on both fronts.

2. Changing Job demands and pressures

It has been found that workloads, new job structures and demands especially in the IT industry and service industries have pressurised employees to be present at their work places for greater lengths of time Ishaya and Ayman (2008). Morgan (2003) further argues that the predominance of the internet and use of mobile phones has allowed organisations to be constantly in touch with their employees 24 by 7.

Most studies show that since the last twenty-five years work has considerably increased. This increase is attributed for the most part to the information technology revolution and in part because of a change in organisations work culture which today encourages severe, cut-throat work performance based environments that expects employees to deliver more and more yet provides very little safety in return as against the old regime which encouraged long-standing loyalty and a sense of corporate community.

For the working population the pressures at work have been escalating over the last few decades. Factors like the need to respond quickly to issues in the workplace, the weightage attached to providing quality customer service and the ramifications on the employee who is expected to be constantly available and eager to serve, all put stress on the employee and demand adjustments in both time and interference in personal space.

As roles, work and the business environment have transformed considerably over the last two decades in India; this has brought about a change in general life roles too. There was a time when people went to work from Monday to Saturday and worked a typical eight-nine hours a day. The borders between home and work domains were clearer, however today the scenario is different, things have changed and, unfortunately, the borders have become indistinct for many employees, resulting in increased stress and burnout.

3. The Changing concept of the 'Family'

The traditional customary family model consisting of the 'breadwinner' father, 'homemaker' mother and children is already a redundant concept in the Western countries (Nieva, 1985; Burley, 1995; Lewis and Cooper, 1995; Burke, 1997). Women's and men's roles in the family are shifting radically (Cowerman, 1989; Burley, 1995; Lewis and Cooper, 1995; Burke, 1997). There are many people who are accepting lesser salaries or income so that they get more hours at home with the family and can attain a better balanced life (Lewis and Cooper, 1995).

These changes in the concept of family and family structures tend to affect men and women differently (Burke and Greenglass, 1989; Gallos, 1989), but effects are generally more pronounced for women (Cowerman, 1989; Burley, 1995; Lewis and Cooper, 1995; Burke, 1997). Added to this is the fact that the joint family system in India is slowly disappearing and is an almost redundant concept in urban India, hence traditional support systems have gradually disappeared. Families have become nuclear where both the spouses go to work (Patel 2005), and despite more women entering the formal labour market, household tasks, chores and caring responsibilities are still predominantly performed by women (Singh 2004).

4. Other issues

This paper has not delved into the economic issues facing India like general poverty, illiteracy and unemployment, a lot has been written and discussed about these problems which are significant contributors to the plight of women in India. Another subject of interest is the role of media in creating and propagating gender role stereotypes in society, which is also a key concern today with the proliferation of various media across India to even the smallest villages. However, the focus of this discourse would not be able to do justice to these issues and remain faithful to the subject that forms the crux of this paper therefore a mention and acknowledgment seems essential before moving on to the solutions.

What can be done?

There cannot be a single solution for the issue of inclusion, women empowerment or gender roles perception, there are many stakeholders and each set of stakeholders needs to play a role in ensuring that these issues are not neglected and are addressed in a proper way. In the following paragraphs three major stakeholders viz, organizations and government and society have been outlined, these suggestions are adapted from recommendations of various bodies, committees and panels including The United Nations Human Rights Commission, The Convention on the Elimination of All Forms of Discrimination against Women (CEDAW), International Organisation for Economic Co-operation and Development (OECD) International Labour Organization (ILO) etc.

The role of the society and government:

1. The influence of gender roles can be seen everywhere, especially when it comes to the decisions that women take regarding their education, careers, family, children and fertility, and work. Whether it is the government or society

in general a change in perceptions is long overdue. These changes could start at government level with developing programmes aimed at elimination of gender stereotypes, awareness campaigns right from school level and curriculum development that includes topics on gender sensitivity and awareness.

Alleviation of discriminatory social norms with respect to women's unpaid work especially in the care sector is crucial this can be done by accentuating and trying to change attitudes in society that places the chief responsibility for the home, child and elderly care on women and girls.

2. Economic independence: To give women a greater level of control over their lives economic independence is a must, earning a living is a primary way to achieve this, however, since women still continue to bear an unequal quantity ot home and care responsibilities, many women still feel compelled to choose between home and career.

   Tax incentives could be offered to women and organisations which would encourage more hiring of women and also enhance women's empowerment and representation in industry.

3. Equal pay for equal work is a principal that is upheld by the government and its policies despite this the gender pay gap remains. The root causes of which boils down to the gap connecting women's educational achievements and afterwards their professional progress. Another cause for the gap in pay is that women typically find employment in only certain sectors where they remain over-represented such as health care, education and administration. Also it has been found that women feel compelled to leave the labour force during

parenthood which then in the long run affects their entire working lives from pay, promotions, career advancement and pensions.

4. Legislation: Though there are laws against gender bias or discrimination both at the workplace and in other fields. It is still seen that discrimination exists at all levels. An effective legal framework which includes appraisal, monitoring and enforcement, as well as exchange of ideas with business, NGO's and equality bodies, such as that are present in many developed nations is a must.

   Ratifying laws that change societal perceptions against gender-based violence, including issues such as domestic violence, sexual harassment at the work place and more serious offences like rape. Also increasing the rate and speed of convictions, should help in changing the mind sets of what is socially permitted and what masculinity means in these contexts.

   Passing laws on inheritance of property, control of financial assets and dilution or scrapping of archaic laws that promote discrimination against women and girls in the family, which prevents them from getting what is their legal right.

5. Correcting the misconceptions and representations of women in Media and its content at all levels, media content that objectifies women and creates the wrong images and consequently stereotypes should be strictly reviewed and discouraged.

6. Encouragement should be given to women to participate and take on leadership roles in religious community groups. This would lead to higher levels of gender sensitivity.

The role of Organisations/Employers:

1. **Concept of 'One size fits all' will not work:** Human Resource Professionals and organisations have to get over the idea of solutions that are based on the concept of 'one size fits all'. People's needs change with time and the same person may require different things at different times for example; Position in the Life cycle is one such consideration. i.e. a bachelor's needs are different from a middle aged working mother or from a young single father etc, most Human resource initiatives are still based on the 'factory' concept of work when everything was uniform and coordinated this assumption cannot work anymore.

   When human resource professionals devise policies and guidelines to tackle issues such as retention, satisfaction, morale, and productivity in the workplace, inputs that consider other facets of an employee's life including the changing nature of what constitutes 'family' warrants serious consideration.

2. Human resource departments must start to think differently in an ideal case scenario development of an 'enabling framework' within organisations is a must, in this policies and development processes should be frequently assessed and modified so as to remove any biases against women, starting from recruitment and including policies on pay and promotion

3. Commitment from Top Management to set the right tone in the organisation for a gender positive culture which includes changing mind-sets, proactively pursuing change management introduction of gender sensitisation training and removing perceptions related to stereotyping of women and their roles and abilities, this will help to reduce culture based biases.

4. Gender should be treated as a core issue in business strategy, this means inclusion of women specific issues but tempered with measurable targets and accountability so as to avoid failure.
5. Building and developing support systems that empower women, not just from within the organisations themselves but also partnering with external agencies could also be considered, so as to aid women and help them achieve an even playing field where responsibilities could be shared or help could be sought.
6. Helping to enable women to network freely along with men, without feeling any form of stigma that could be associated with interacting with colleagues after work. A positive step in this direction could be mentoring programmes with other successful women.

Conclusion

If women's workforce participation rates are to increase it requires the dynamic support, contribution and involvement of all major stakeholders' right from the society and government to employers and the family unit to remove or reduce gender insensitivity, stereotyping and biases towards women and their roles.

If the concepts of 'work' and 'family 'have changed, and probably will continue to change in the future, Indian society also has to accept that gender roles and definitions should also change to meet the need of the hour.

Inflexible definitions and perceptions regarding gender roles can hinder individual choices and limit potentials of not only women but men also. Supporting unbiased and non discriminatory views of gender roles right from education, career choice and at the workplace has become imperative if India wants to progress and compete with the developed nations of the world.

References

Abele, A. (2003). The dynamics of masculine-agentic and feminine-communal traits: Findings from a prospective study. *Journal of Personality and Social Psychology*, 85, 768–776.

Anderson, M. (1988). Thinking about women: Sociological perspectives on sex and gender (2nd ed.). New York: Macmillan Publishing Company

Banyard, K. (2010). The equality illusion: The truth about women and men today. Faber & Faber.

Brett, J. M., & Stroh, L. K. (1997). Jumping ship: Who benefits from an external labor market career strategy? Journal of Applied Psychology, 82, 331–341

Burke, R. J., & Greenglass, E. R. (1989). Psychological burnout among men and women in teaching: An examination of the Cherniss model. *Human Relations*, 42(3), 261-273.

Burke, R. J.: 1997, Are Families Damaging to Careers?, Women in Management Review 13(8), 320–324.

Burley, K. A. (1995). Family variables as mediators of the relationship between work-family conflict and marital adjustment among dual-career men and women. *The Journal of Social Psychology*, 135(4), 483-497.

Catalyst (2008). 2008 Catalyst Census of Women Corporate Officers and Top Earners of the FP500 . Available at http://www.catalyst.org/system/files/cote_ca_09.pdf. Accessed on 30/06/2017

Catalyst (2016) Catalyst: Quick Take; Women in the labour Force in India, New York Catalyst 2017. Available at http://www.catalyst.org/knowledge/women-labour-force-india#footnoteref26_2hft59c. Accessed on 30/06/2017

Confederation of Indian Industry, (2009) "Understanding the Levels of Empowerment of Women in the Workplace in India"

Cowerman, S. (1989) 'Role overload, role conflict, and stress: Addressing consequences of multiple role demands, Social Forces, 67(4) 965-82.

Credit Suisse Diversity on Board! Published: 10.06.2015 Available at :https://www.credit-suisse.com/corporate/en/articles/news-and-expertise/diveristy-on-board-201506.html Accessed on 12/03/2016

Diekman, A. B., & Eagly, A. H. (2000). Stereotypes as dynamic constructs: Women and men of the past, present, and future. *Personality and Social Psychology Bulletin*, 26, 1171–1188.

Eagly, A. H., & Karau, S. J. (2002). Role congruity theory of prejudice toward female leaders. *Psychological Review*, 109(3), 573–598

Eagly, A. H., & Steffen, V. J. (1984). Gender stereotypes stem from the distribution of women and men into social roles. *Journal of personality and social psychology*, *46*(4), 735.

Gallos, J. V. (1989). 6 Exploring women's development: implications for career theory, practice. *Handbook of career theory*, 110.

Heilman, M. E. (1983). Sex bias in work settings: The lack of fit model. In Staw, B., & Cummings, L. Eds. Research in organizational behavior (Vol. 5). Greenwich, CT: JAI.

Heilman, M. E. (2001). Description and prescription: How gender stereotypes prevent women's ascent up the organizational ladder. Journal of Social Issues, 57(4), 657–674.

Heilman, M. E., & Chen, J. J. (2005). Same behavior, different consequences: Reactions to men's and women's altruistic citizenship behavior. Journal of Applied Psychology, 90, 431–441.

Heilman, M. E., & Okimoto, T. G. (2007). Why are women penalized for success at male tasks?: The implied communality deficit. Journal of Applied Psychology, 92, 81–92.

Heilman, M. E., & Parks-Stamm, E. J. (2007). Gender stereotypes in the workplace: Obstacles to women's career progress. In Correll, S. J. (Ed.). Social Psychology of Gender: Advances in Group Processes. Vol. 24 (pp.47–77). Elsevier Ltd., JAI Press

ILO: Beyond the "glass ceiling": Women in the world of work progress, but slowly: 2001 originally published in World of work, No. 39, June 2001, Geneva ILO, 2007

Indian Census 2011, Chapter 6 (State of Literacy), p.14" . *Government of India.*

International Organisation for Economic Co-operation and Development International Labour Organization https://www.oecd.org/g20/topics/employment-and-social-policy/Monitoring-progress-in-reducing-the-gender-gap-in-labour-force-participation.pdf

Ishaya, N., & Ayman, R. (2008). Predicting work-family conflict via perceived involvement and overload. *American Psychological Association*, Boston, MA, USA.

Johnston, W. B. (1987). *Workforce 2000: Work and workers for the 21st century*. Government Printing Office.

Kelly Services, Inc (2016) Kelly Global Workforce Insights (KGWI) survey on Women in STEM - How and why an inclusive strategy is critical to closing the STEM talent gap. Available online at http://www.kellyocg.com/siteassets/7-kellyocg/uploadedfiles/7-kellyocg/2-knowledge /workforce_trends /womeninstem_ kgwi.pdf. Accessed on 20/03/2017.

Koshal, Manjulika, Koshal, Rajindar K. & Gupta, Ashok (2006). Women managers in India: challenges and opportunities. In Management in India: Trends and Transition/edited by Herbert J. Davis, Samir R. Chatterjee and Mark Heuer. New Delhi, Response Books, 2006.

Kulkarni S.S. (2002). Women and Professional Competency- A Survey Report, *Indian Journal of Training and Development*. 32(2) April-June 4

Lewis, S., & Cooper, C. L. (1995). Balancing the work/home interface: A European perspective. *Human Resource Management Review, 5*(4), 289-305.

McKinsey Global Institute (2015). The power of parity: advancing women's equality in India McKinsey & Company 2015 Available at http://www.mckinsey.com/search?q=india%20gender%20gap accessed on 25/03/2017

Mehra, P. (2002). Women Managers: To the top and Beyond, Hindu Businessline, Saturday, 27 April

Morgan, H. (2003). The challenges of a global marketplace. In Human Resources in the 21st century, ed. M. Goldsmith, R. Gandossy, and M. Effron. New York: Wiley.

Nieva, V. F. (1985). Work and family linkages. *Women and work: An annual review, 1*, 162-190.

Patel, T. (2005). The family in India: Structure and practice. New Delhi: Sage.

Peterson, V., & Runyan, A. (1999). Global gender issues. Boulder: Westview Press.

Rudman, L. A. (1998). Self-promotion as a risk factor for women: The costs and benefits of counter-stereotypical impression management. *Journal of Personality and Social Psychology*, 74, 629–645.

Singh, B. (2004). Working women in India. New Delhi: Anmol.

Singh, J. P. (2002). Social and cultural aspects of gender inequality and discrimination in India. *Asian Profile,* 30(2):163–176.

Singh, K. (2003). Women managers: perception v/s performance analysis, *Journal of Management Research,* 3 (1), pp 31-42

The Convention on the Elimination of All Forms of Discrimination against Women (CEDAW) Available at http://www.un.org/womenwatch/daw/cedaw/recommendations/ accessed on 27/03/2017

The European Commission. (March, 2011). The European Commission's new gender equality study: Towards quotas for women in the board room. Frankfort, Germany: European Central Bank Diversity Forum.

United Nations Human Rights Commission Report Available at http://www.ohchr.org/EN/Issues/Women/WRGS/Pages/GenderStereotypes.aspx accessed on 27/03/2017

Varma, R. (2002). Women in information technology: A case study of undergraduate students in a minority-serving institution. *Bulletin of Science, Technology, and Society,* 22(4):274– 282.

World Bank (2017) available at http://data.worldbank.org/indicator/SL.TLF.CACT.FE.ZS accessed on 27/03/2017

4

Women Empowerment and Entrepreneurship: A Case Study of Shri Mahila Griha Udyog Lijjat Papad

Shelly de (Pandit)

Introduction

The concept of Women empowerment was introduced at the Nairobi International Women Conference, 1985 which defined it as 'redistribution of social power and control of resources in favour of women'. Women empowerment actually refers to multi dimensional activities which includes individual's act of expressing or defending rights, claims, or opinions in a way to achieve basic power and to establish full identity of women. On the other hand women empowerment is a process, which encompasses different aspects to enhance awareness and increase access to resources. Thus, Women empowerment is concerned with the gaining of autonomy and control over resources, which includes many dimensions such as economic, social and political. Koko, 1992, said that empowerment of women means developing them as more aware individuals, who are politically active, economically productive and independent and are able to make intelligent discussion in matters that affect them.

The process of empowerment has five dimensions, viz. cognitive, psychological, economic, political and physical (Mokta, 2014). When women have economically and socially independence, they will be able to take firm decisions against their oppression in families and society. They can integrate their needs for empowerment and motives for empowerment. Thus, empowerment of women refers to the ability of women to enjoy their rights to control and benefit from resources as well as the ability to control risk and improve their economic status and wellbeing.

The Oxford Living dictionaries define entrepreneurship as 'A person who sets up a business or businesses, taking on financial risks in the hope of profit'. Thus entrepreneurship is a process to learn how to manage an organisation with available assets and resources and how to control it. Entrepreneurship contributed a major role in the economic and social growth of a country. It is the term which is directly associated with women empowerment by not only generating self-employment opportunity in the present social system in our country but also creating economic and social independence among women.

The United Nation's Women's Empowerment Principles, Equality means Business, 2010 offer practical guidance to business and the private sector on how to empower women in the workplace, marketplace and community. Developed through a partnership between UN Women and the United Nations Global Compact, the Principles are designed to support companies in reviewing existing policies and practices—or establishing new ones—to realize women's empowerment. In brief, the Principles are:

1. Establish high-level corporate leadership for gender equality
2. Treat all women and men fairly at work—respect and support human rights and nondiscrimination

3. Ensure the health, safety and well-being of all women and men workers
4. Promote education, training and professional development for women
5. Implement enterprise development, supply chain and marketing practices that empower women
6. Promote equality through community initiatives and advocacy
7. Measure and publicly report on progress to achieve gender equality (www.unwomen.org)

Objectives

The objective of this study is to find out the contribution of women entrepreneurship of Shri Mahila Griha Udyog Lijjat Papad (SMGULP) towards economic and social empowerment of women. It will also explore the success story of women entrepreneurism of Lijjat Papad from a mere cottage industry to a symbol of women empowerment.

Methodology

The present study is descriptive in nature. It is based on secondary data only. Secondary data is collected from Annual reports, books, journals, relevant websites and previous research findings.

Review of Literature

Bhatnagar (2003) SMGULP is an organization that has acted as a catalyst in empowering poor urban women across India during the last four decades. Remuneration is the same for everyone, and profits and losses are shared equally among the member sisters, so there is no possibility of concentration of assets and wealth. Lijjat refuses to accept donations, but instead provides donations to the needy.

DAC Network on Gender Equality (GENDERNET) (2011) disclosed that the largest share of bilateral aid to gender equality and women's empowerment in the economic and productive sectors. Economic empowerment increases women's access to economic resources and opportunities including jobs, financial services, property and other productive assets, skills development and market information.

Rahman and Sultana (2012), in their study focused on contribution of SMGULP on social development of Women. The primary data was collected through structured questionnaire from 60 respondents of SMGULP Society in Hyderabad District. They found that the development of Shri Mahila Griha Udyog Lijjat Papad should be taken in broader framework of women empowerment. The organization is responsible for empowering women by the way of promoting self –reliance, self-confident, self-dependent and educating them to realize their fundamental rights. Lijjat has made women financially stable to such an extent that after taking their rightful share for their livelihood, they are contributing generously to societal cause.

Sharma et al (2012) said that Women entrepreneur networks are major sources of knowledge about women's entrepreneurship and they are increasingly recognized as a valuable tool for its development and promotion. This will motivate other rural women to engage in micro entrepreneurship with the right assistance and they can strengthen their capacities besides adding to the family income and national productivity.

Rawat et al (2013) found that Lijjat Papad is an exceptionally successful story of entrepreneurship. What merely started as a small scale cottage industry became a corporate giant merely within four decades and is still growing. It is looked upon as an ideal by every entrepreneur in today's time. This brand is a special one because it makes a difference in the livelihood of thousands of poor women in India.

Rani (2016) said that in developing country like India, SMGULP is a symbol of progress. The managers can pick up an interesting lesson from SMGULP which is holding its core values from the past 56 years i.e. the concept of business adopted by the organization for empowering the women which deals in producing qualitated products at reasonable price. It provides employment to around 43,000 (in 2015) women. The economic empowerment is not only the aim of the organization but it makes the women self-confident and self-reliant and uplifts their standard of living.

Analysis and Findings

- **The Success Story of Lijjat**

Shri Mahila Griha Udyog Lijjat Papad (SMGULP) is an incredible example of women entrepreneurship making women economically and socially empowered in our country. The story was started on 15th March, 1959, when 7 women of Girguam of South Mumbai were gathered on the terrace of the building and produced 4 packets of Papads to sell to their neighborhood. They eventually sold all those packets and resolved a firm decision to continue the production of papad. Within a very short period of time the membership started growing from the initial 7 members and become ever-increasing. In this way the organisation started growing. But the early days to run the business were not so easy. They did not have enough money to start it. They had to borrow a sum of Rs 80/- to start the new venture. The turning point was taken place in 1966 when it was registered under the Bombay Public Trust Act 1950 and also registered under Societies Registration Act, 1860 and got recognition from Khadi & Village Industries Commission as a village industry.

The journey of the 7 members - organisation now becomes more than 43000 members. These members are called Bens or sisters. The wide-spread organisation with it's Central Office at Mumbai presently has 81 Branches and 27 Divisions in different states all over India (source-lijjat.com). Every branch is headed by a Sanchalika to see the production of the branch. All the branches are autonomous units and the income or loss as the case may be of such unit is borne by the owner sister members of that branch by increasing or decreasing their rolling charges accordingly. So, all of the members are the owners of the organisation. The success to become the mammoth and successful organisation with an annual turnover of Rs. 6.5 billion is fully based on the combined efforts and the commitment of it's Bens. They may not have formal education but have belief in 'the strength of a woman'. The organisation is now manufacturing several products from its world famous Papad to Appalam, Masala, Gehu Atta, Chapati, SASA Detergent Powder, SASA Detergent Cake (Tikia) and SASA Liquid Detergent (source-lijjat.com). It's exports are made through Merchant Exporters to countries like UK, USA, Middle East Countries, Thailand, Singapore, Hongkong, Holland, Japan, Australia and other Countries. Current export amount of l;ijjat Papad is Rs. 100 million (www.lijjat.com)

The basic three-tier concepts on which the organisation is developed are-

(1) The concept of Business

(2) The concept of family

(3) The concept of Devotion,

These entire concepts are completely and uniformly followed in the organisation. The concept of business is to produce quality goods at reasonable price. Lijjat has never and nor will it in the future, accept any charity, donation, gift or grant from any quarter but the member sisters donate collectively for good causes from time to time according to their capacity. The concept of family is the mutual family affection where trust and concern are two basic things. The third concept – 'concept of devotion' is the most important one as the Bens belief that Lijjat is not only a palce of earning rather a place of devotion and worship. As an entrepreneur the Bens learned the three tier system to run the organisation.

The following diagram represents the organisational structure of SMGULP-

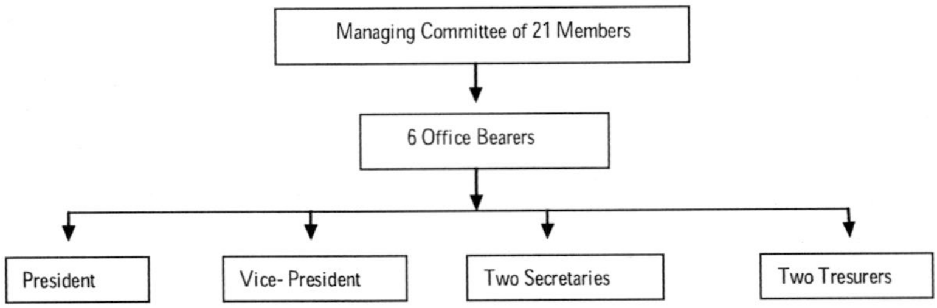

Diagram-1

Source-www.lijjat.com

SMGULP has a Central Managing Committee, which consist of 21 members out of, which we have 6 (Six) elected Office Bearers i.e. President, Vice - President, Two Secretaries and Two Treasurers to run the organisation smoothly.

The institution got many awards like 'Power Brand 2010-2011' by the Indian Consumer, the Economic Times Award for Corporate Excellence "Business Woman of the Year", 2000-2001, 'Best Village Industry Institution' by Khadi & Village Industries Commission along with Ministry of Agro and Rural Industries, 2003 etc. Lijjat was featured in various T.V. Channels, which include BBC World in the programme "**Business Bizarre**".

- **SMGULP and Socio - Economic Empowerment of Women**

SMGULP is a women's organisation which has defined the mechanism for women's development to bring in individual and collective empowerment through improvement in both 'condition' and 'position' of women (Rahman 2012). So this organisaton is 'of the women, by the women and for the women'. The main objective of SMGULP is to provide employment to women to enable them to earn decent and dignified livelihood. The essence of women economic empowerment is the rights to control and benefit from resources, assets and income. In SMGULP the entrepreneurship not only helped these illiterate or semi-educated women of the society to earn money but also empowering them with employable skills by giving training. This organisation is working on the same principle which was suggested by UNDP, 2008 as 'Providing supplementary services – such as training, working through groups rather than individuals, or alongside other investments in awareness raising – has been shown to increase women's direct control over resources '.

As an entrepreneur the commitment to maintain the quality of products not only increased the business of SMGULP but it also enhanced the value and morale of women. In SMGULP no member women are considered as worker of the organisation rather they enjoy the right of ownership. Thus all members of the organisation are the owner of the company. The contribution of orgânization to the economic empowerment of women is in the form of earning through daily working (mainly Papad rolling). The organisation is proving literacy to its members and also taking the responsibility to educate their children. These Bens understood that literacy is the key factor for a society and realized that collective empowerment through 'condition' and 'position' of women can play a lead role to earn self respect and reliance in the society. The organisation provides scholarships to the children of the sister-members who pass out in 10th and 12th standard every year so as to enable the women of SMGULP to encourage their children for education.

In SMGULP, the sisterhood system taught them how to share profit and losses equally and the concept of equal remuneration. So there is no possibility of concentration of assets and wealth for a particular sister. Each branch enjoys autonomy and thus the member sisters realized the true meaning of independence. This independence helped them to achieve social independence. SMGULP has a committee of 21 that decides how the profits are to be distributed. They generally buy gold coins - 5gm or 10 gm, depending on the profit. Everyone gets an equal share of profit, irrespective of who does what work, irrespective of seniority or responsibility. In this way the organisation helped its sister-membes to acquire assets. Lijjat never took any charity or donations. In this way it teaches its sister-member to earn self respect and self-dignity.

The success of the organisation is based on Gandian philosophy of Sarvodaya which means 'universal uplift' or 'progress of all'. At the same time, each and every member has the veto power. All decisions, major or minor, are based on consensus among members. Any single member's objection can nullify a decision. As an entrepreneur they participate in the decision making process and actually learned the art of leadership which is a very important part of socio-economic empowerment.

The entrepreneurship in Lijjat enabled women to achieve their Social empowerment in the way of increasing their self-confidence individually and collectively to change their social status. These Bens learned what is self-esteem, self-confidence and Lijjat has made them aware to for a better future. At SMGULP, the entrepreneur-sisters are becoming socially empowered by improving their skills, knowledge and self-perception.

Thus SMGULP is a story of women entrepreneurship. Ex-President of SMGULP, Vimlaben once said that that "the objective is to maximize employment opportunities for women through activities connected with village industries, while, at the same time, not sacrificing basic business principles and quality consciousness. We are a full-fledged commercial, self reliant organisation and not a charitable society" (www.lijjat.com). On 21st December 2005 SMGULP had received the 'Brand Equity Award' from the then president of India for its superior quality products.

As the entrepreneur the members of SMGULP learned how to run the business process smoothly, or how to share profit equally, how to clear agent's due within the stipulated period of time, how to assure the consumers that they get the assurance of quality at a good price. The monthly regional meetings, annual general meetings, and All-India conventions of branches are held to keep the members aware of organizational activities and strategies. *Lijjat Patrika,* the in-house magazine, is published and circulated among members for a strong communication. In this way Lijjat has taken a holistic approach for its entrepreneur-sisters' social and economic empowerment.

Conclusions

Women empowerment is a continuous process. Lijjat is the story of successful women entrepreneurship in our country. From the inception, SMGULP has played an important role to empower women socially and economically by promoting self–reliance, self-confident, self-dependent and by providing education to its sisters-members to realize their fundamental rights. Started with a modest loan of Rs 80, the cooperative now has annual sales exceeding Rs 6.50 billion. It is an organization that has acted as a catalyst in empowering poor urban women across India during the last 58 years. It begins with a small group of 7 women in 1959 and today Lijjat has more than 43,000 members in 81 branches across 27 divisions in different states all over India (lijjat.com). SMGULP is a women's organisation manufacturing various products from Ppad, Appalam, Masala to Detergent. Remuneration is the same for everyone, and profits and losses are shared equally among the member sisters, so there is no possibility of concentration of assets and wealth. Lijjat refuses to accept donations, but instead provides donations to the needy. The success of the organisation is based on Gandian philosophy of Sarvodaya and from the efforts of its member sisters who have withstood several hardships with unshakable belief in 'the strength of a woman' and thus empowered themselves socially and economically. SMGULP has helped its Bens financially and socially stable in such a way that after taking their rightful share for their livelihood, they are contributing generously to societal cause. The members are now economically and socially enough empowered to realize their full identity and power in all spheres of life. Women empowerment may have a lot of goals but the main motto is to recognize the contribution of women in the growth of a nation and SMGULP through its entrepreneur-sisters has fulfilled this aim successfully.

References

1. https://en.oxforddictionaries.com/definition/entrepreneur
2. Koko U, "Empowering People for Health and Family Planning", *IASSI Quarterly*, Vol.11, p. 2, 1992
3. Mokta M, 'Empowerment of Women In India: A Critical Analysis", Indian Journal Of Public Administration 474 / Vol. Lx, No. 3, July-September 2014
4. Rahman And Sultana, "Empowerment Of Women For Social Development (A Case Study Of Shri Mahila Griha Udyog Lijjat Papad,Hyderabad District)", Journal of Arts, Science & Commerce, Vol.– III, Issue–3(1),July. 2012 , E-ISSN 2229-46862
5. Rani A, "Women spirit wins: A case study of Lijjat Papad", International Journal of Applied Research 2016; 2(2): 297-302
6. Rawat, Pant & Palit, "A Case Study on Entrepreneurial Journey of Lijjat Papad", EXCEL International Journal of Multidisciplinary Management Studies, Vol.3 (3), March (2013), ISSN 2249- 8834
7. Sharma et al, "Micro Enterprise Development and Rural Women Entrepreneurship: Way for Economic Empowerment", Arth Prabhand: A Journal of Economics and Management Vol.1 Issue 6, September , 2012
8. siteresources.worldbank.org/INTEMPOWERMENT/Resources/14652_Lijjat-web.pdf

9. The United Nation's Women's Empowerment Principles, Equality means Business, 2010

10. UNDP (United Nations Development Programme) (2008), Innovative approaches to promoting women's economic empowerment: paper for the partnership event on September 25, 2008: MDG3 – gender equality and empowerment of women – a prerequisite for achieving all the MDGs by 2015 (New York, 2008), UNDP, New York.

11. www.lijjat .com

12. www.oecd.org/dac/gender-development/47561694.pdf

13. www.unwomen.org

14. www.5wwc.org

5

Outsourcing Social Reproduction, Making them 'Other' Continued Exclusion of the Internal Migrant Women

Saswati Ghosh

As women's work participation outside home has risen, so the need for outsourcing familial responsibilities has expanded. Who will shoulder those responsibilities? Housework has been traditionally defined by patriarchy as women's responsibility, and so when it comes as a paid option, its usually women who have been in charge of that. Obviously, they will be lesser-paid women from relatively poorer households. Domestic workers, working in cities and towns of South Asia are internal migrants – not from other countries, but from rural, often less developed and poorer areas within domestic boundaries. This pattern is also found in Latin American countries to Saudi Arabia or even in Sweden, with the difference there women come from across borders (REF). The usual feature is that these women do not count as workers. But internal migrants face tremendous risks of labour exploitation and unfair recruitment practices. Policymakers usually give importance to cross-border movement, but the intra-country movement of workers is far more significant than cross-border immigration.1 In general, people from poor households move shorter distances because they possess limited resources, networks, market information and skills.3

This paper will look into the internal migrant women, how the responsibility of social reproduction is being outsourced by the 'other' women and society in general, but without any recognition as workers. Apart from that, it will also look in to the internal migrant women, causes and consequences of migration, the push and pull factors, the areas of concentration and "otherisation" of these women in the process, with the denial of political, economic and social rights, often along with apprehensions and allegations of criminal activities attached with them.

Migration literature traditionally conceptualized women as accompanying dependents and without any agency of their own, they were given limited attention in theoretical accounts of migration (Chant and Radcliffe 1992). However, it has since been realised that the causes and consequences of migration in many contexts are different for males and females (Sandbergen 1995). Woman migrating as passive followers of male household heads is increasingly being challenged in new research. Women themselves are going for better opportunities, to negotiate lack of livelihood and poverty in the source place, single daughters of the family are being sent to towns from an early age to enable them to find independent economic opportunities, or avail of newer outlets of education and training. This way 'autonomous female migration' is now an accepted trend (Bhatt 2009). Migration has often been viewed as an individual strategy and related to personal characteristics of the migrant like demographic attributes, lifecycle stage, attachment to a particular place, social capital etc. Others theorised migration decision-making to be a family-based decision, since members of a family usually move together, and gender used to plays a passive role in both views (Chawla, GRDFT Monograph).

Who is a migrant?

In India, one of the major sources of economic data, NSSO, defined migrants as persons 'whose last place of usual residence, anytime in the past, was different from the place of enumeration'. That definition estimated 327.7 million internal migrants in 2008 were comprised of almost 80% women migrants. Out of that 80%, 66.6 million, i.e. 1/5th, were labour migrants (IDRC CDRI, quoted in Chawla). Accounting for just under one-fifth of all internal migrants, and women were estimated to represent 15% of this working population on the move, across both rural and urban India. The NSSO data, however, show that women's migration within India is primarily the result of (a) marriage, with women relocating to join the household of their husband or (b) associational migration where women move as members of a migrating family.

Available reports, micro studies and surveys have questioned this narrow picture painted by government statistics as it fails to grasp the complexity of both the scale and motives of women who migrate for reasons other than the two mentioned above, or who may enter the labour force after migrating as a member of a migrating household. Above all, due to the way 'internal migrants' are defined in terms of place of last residence, official figures exclude large numbers of both men and women who migrate on a temporary basis and thereby do not change residence, and the official definition fails to adequately capture the extent of internal migration in India.

Here we may mention Thadani and Todaro as they describe four principle types of female migrants, distinguished by their marital status and reasons for migrating (Chawla, GEPDF: 2014). These are:

1. Married women migrating for employment
2. Unmarried women migrating for employment
3. Unmarried women migrating for marriage
4. Married women who are engaged in associational Migration.

They can be broadly categorised in two ways, depending on the risks involved: (i) Women migrating independently, i.e., without men and (ii) Women migrating with men.

The bulk of labour migration within India is temporary and circular in nature, and driven by persistent rural and urban poverty, despite marked economic growth at the national level. Rural India is characterized by high rates of unemployment/underemployment, as agricultural wage work has become increasingly scarce and opportunities for diversification of work has become slim. A large portion of the population of India and an even larger proportion of women survives on agriculture. The trend of stagnation in the agrarian economy has contributed to 'feminisation' of migration. According to official statistics, female migration rates for both rural and urban India registered a phenomenal increase between 1993 and 2007-08, even as male migration rates fell and moved towards stagnation in rural areas after an initial increase in urban centres (IDRC/ CDRI, Policy brief 8).

Economic status or poverty plays different roles in male and female migration. As Mahapatro (REF) mentions that studies found economic status of a household has an inverse relation with female migration, while it increases the chances of male. Also women's migration from Northern Ghana show that households resort to migration in response to worsening of agriculture based livelihoods (ILO, 2013). To overcome economic vulnerabilities like lack of employment opportunities and insufficient income, or the inability to meet the economic needs of family members, households (head of household) might decide to migrate either with the entire family, or to diversify its economically active members to different places. Thus it may be a family decision or an individual decision. This enables remittances sent by migrants to help the family members left behind and overcome economic vulnerability. Declining economic opportunities particularly increases the risk of poverty among female-headed households and therefore, female-headed households or single females without any male bread-earner find migration to be the only available method to negotiate economic difficulties.

Internal migrant women: How many?

Given the data available by NSSO, it has already been mentioned that 327.7 million internal migrants in 2008 comprised of almost 80% women migrants. Out of that 80%, 66.6 million, i.e. 1/5th, were labour migrants (IDRC CDRI). On the other hand, calculating from 2001 Census data, there are 309 million migrants based on place of last residence, female migrants constitute 218 million while it is 91 million for males (Mahapatra). By Majumder and Agnihotri's calculation, migrants constitute around 30 percent of the total population; whereas male and female migrants constitute 18 percent and 45 percent of their population respectively. According to the NSS figures, the proportions of women migrating for marriage increased from 25 per cent of the rural female population in 1993 to 38 per cent in 1999–2000 and then to 44 per cent in 2007–08. Increased rates of rural marriage migration is confirmed by census data for the 1990s, and she asks what processes have led to a substantial rise in migration for marriage in rural areas. Running parallel to the remarkable increase in rural female marriage migration is an equally remarkable decline in rural female work participation rates from 33 per cent in 1993-94 to 29 per cent in 2007-08 and further to 26 per cent in 2009-10.17 While rural employment for women is showing signs of acute decline, urban female work participation rates too have declined from 15.5 per cent in 1993–94 to 13.8 per cent in 2007–08 and remained the same in 2009–10. Then rise in migration becomes a riddle we are not getting in to here.

Reasons for Migration according to official data Mahapatra noted that, although in reality a number of factors determine the movement of females from one place to another, such multiple reasons for migration would be too complex to be incorporated in to national level census, and can only be captured trough micro level data. However, Indian Census started collecting information on reasons for migration since 1981 based on place of last residence. The 1981 Census provided data on main reasons for migration in terms of five broad categories, namely, employment, education, family moved, marriage and other reasons. In 1991 Census, business and natural calamities were cited as reasons for migration. Census 2001, provided 7 reasons for migration. Moved at birth has been included in 2001 census as a reason for migration and natural calamities as a reason excluded from it. These definitional changes make comparison across Censuses a problem. The 2011 Census has put the internal migrants figure at 453.6 million, 37% of the total population, of whom 70% are women along the same 7 reasons for migration.

An increasing share of the internal migrant women is joining domestic work for a livelihood. There are strong push and pull factors behind increasing migration. Among the push factors are: deteriorating agricultural economies and declining food production; land scarcity and loss of women's rights to land; changing marital patterns and family situations such as men's outmigration, desertion by husbands, conflicts with in-laws, and female-headed households.4 Domestic work is a principal occupation that a number of women migrants end up doing due to two main reasons: first, it gives an easy foothold into the urban economy as it does not require capital or particular educational preparation; and second, for new arrivals in the city, the opportunity to live in one's employer's house means ready accommodation and safety and security.

There are strong pull factors as well. The increasing participation of urban women in paid employment in private and public sectors, and growth in households headed by women have created a demand for domestic workers. Even in rural areas, women have turned to informal forms of child care, such as engaging other women, from poorer families, to perform their traditionally defined, unpaid, domestic roles within the home.

Lack of access to rights and amenities

The Constitution does not restrict free movement throughout the territory of India, and this guarantee is often used as an excuse to dismiss the difficulties faced by these internal migrants. Internal migrants find it difficult, and are often unable, to claim social protection entitlements due to lack of evidences of identity and residence. They are also excluded from many government sponsored schemes and programmes. Internal migrants, of which nearly 80% are women, are excluded from the economic, cultural, social and political life of society and are often treated as second-class citizens. The constraints faced by migrants are multifarious – lack of formal residency rights; lack of identity proof; lack of political representation; inadequate housing; low-paid, insecure or hazardous work; extreme vulnerability of women and children to trafficking and sex exploitation; exclusion from state-provided services such as health and education and discrimination based on ethnicity, religion, class or gender. On the top of that, the portrayal of migrants as a '*burden*' to the society discourages their settling down, and removes them from urban planning initiatives.

Women migrants, especially those in the lower end informal sector occupations, remain invisible and discriminated against in the workforce. There is lesser representation of female migrants in regular jobs and are on an average, paid less than male migrants and enjoy no maternity benefits. Even trade unions do not recognise them as 'workers' and keep away from organising them for rights. Around 10% of India's GDP is a contribution of circular migrants, or those who come back to their place of origin on a regular basis, as in 2009, the necessity of an inclusive policy focusing on the needs of the migrants thus should become imperative on the policy-makers.(Deshingkar 2009).

The requirement for documentation to access welfare entitlements disproportionately affects women in a negative manner. Asset holding, official documentation and household identification in the name of women are still largely uncommon. Registering women-headed households and single-women households in the case of unmarried women and widows remains a struggle, which often means that such households are also left out of poverty alleviation schemes. In this context, for migrants, accessing food and other basic necessities is difficult and acts as a push towards debt incurred for consumption loans, bringing on further hardship.

Another important right internal migrants tend to lose out on is the exercise of their right to political franchise. Since voting is linked to residence and most migrants do not possess electoral cards in their destination areas, they are often not able to exercise their right to vote unless they are present in their place of origin at the time of elections. Furthermore, migrant communities are a low-priority constituency for those seeking elected office because of prevalent political ideologies and hostility from 'locals', with negative rhetoric often peaking at election time (Chawla, GRFDT).

Women who migrate because of cross-regional marriages face additional vulnerabilities and barriers to accessing their civil rights and entitlements—as well as rights related to property, inheritance and children. To date official registration of legal forms of marriage across regions is not mandatory, despite a clause in CEDAW to this effect, with GOI exercising this as one of the points of reservation. The lack of rights endured by these women, combined with the hardships of being positioned far from their familiar communities, cultures and languages, leaves them more vulnerable, being open to additional pressures, domestic violence (a growing trend in India), economic exploitation and poverty.

Compared to international labour migration, local recruitment is much less regulated, much more informal, and hardly documented. The operations of local recruitment and placement agencies are probably hardly monitored or inspected by governments even though licensing requirements may exist. Informal, unlicensed recruiters most likely outnumber registered agencies. Moreover, because there are few or no formal channels of information regarding available local jobs in domestic work and about job-seekers, and because employment relationships in domestic work tend to be highly personalised, prospective employer and workers often rely on networks of relatives and friends, and on "word of mouth" to facilitate their search (ILO, UNESCO).

A domestic worker from a far-flung village may be as much a stranger in her/his country's city as a migrant worker in another country. He/she might come from a tribe or ethnic group that is different from (and perceived as being of lower status than) the employer's or the city's; speak a different dialect or language; practice a different religion; unable to read or write; and simply be unfamiliar with the practices of urbanised households.

Outsourcing social reproduction

Truong (1996; 2003; 2006) posits that the emergence of women's migration across borders as domestic helpers and sexual service providers constitutes a transfer of reproductive and sexual labour from one social group and nation to another. The same model can be applied to different regions of a country or at a sub-national level. Comparatively wealthier women can engage other poorer/backward/low caste/minority women to carry out the domestic chores. Parreñas (2001) has extended this idea and formulates the concept of the 'international division of reproductive labour' to cover the transfer of care duties between three groups of women: female employers in the receiving countries, migrant workers, and women in the countries of origin who care for those who stay behind. This form of analysis has exposed the chains of negative externalities by which an enhancement of care provision through labour import in some countries can lead to the denial of the entitlement to care of others who have stayed behind.

Contemporary migration chains in this 'intimate' side of the economy operate within a two-tiered system. Tier (1) consists of the care sector in which the chains have been formed by a combination of macro and meso institutional factors. These include the care deficit in major industrialized countries caused by ageing populations, structural reforms affecting the quality and coverage of care, and the growth of women's participation in the labour force without a corresponding rise in the range and intensity of men's 'domestic' participation. Tier (2) consists of the commercial sex sector, which has evolved with a different set of dynamics. These came about through the growth of tourism driven by the desire for foreign exchange earnings, combined with the political will to allow commercial sexual services to become integrated with tourism (Truong 1990).

This neglect of social reproduction takes care as a moral duty, and of sex as intimacy, which refuses to recognize that the liberalization of economies and broadening market relations can free up a social and moral space for care and sexual services to become incorporated into (semi-industrial) labour relations (Truong 2016). Growing links between different national systems of social reproduction, now spanning most countries and regions, are being formed, and point to the formation of a new class of women based on their gender identity (female), their work (domestic helper, commercial sexual provider, foreign bride), and their unrecognized status in migration law (Truong 2016). The socio-legal space through which these migratory movements take place is ambiguous and therefore abuse is frequent and often without redress.

Domestic worker migrants are very largely women, including in the case of Indonesia where they form by far the largest part of an emigrant labour force which, by 2010, was sending remittances equal to eleven per cent of the country's gross domestic product. Rich countries increasingly depend for their social and family reproduction on migrant women's labour for a range of demanding or 'menial' tasks that their own populations are less willing to undertake: cleaning, cooking, childcare, and care of the sick and of the old. The large movement of women in rich and middle-income countries into paid employment, while the numbers of old people steeply rise, is based to a large extent on the ability to hire poorer women (and men) to undertake these tasks, whether women from their own country or – increasingly – women from poor countries who are drawn to richer locations by the low level of opportunities in their home places, the high expectations placed on them for support for family members, the hopes raised by successful examples, and the promises circulated by migration industry brokers. The social reproduction of rich countries (and rich people in middle- and low-income countries), in all the cycles of daily living and generational rise and fall, physical and emotional maintenance, is highly dependent on 'domestic workers' who are largely not recognized and protected as 'workers', and whose own physical and emotional maintenance is stressed and often violated.

While domestic work is a relatively easy entry sector, many interviews recount the advantage that some employers take of their 'irregular' employees, and how migrants may thus after a while move on again to less oppressive and humiliating work, if and when they see a possibility. Related to this they may seek to regularize their status. Thai economy's hunger for cheap dependent Burmese labour and Thai society's predominant comprehensive hostility to the labourers and their families can be a good example of this duality (REF)

Lao and Thailand: Making women domestic workers invisible

How women domestic workers are denied rights or safety can be found from policy regimes in Laos and Thailand. Although around 60% of migrants from Laos (the Lao People's Democratic Republic) to Thailand have been women, a new migration policy regime formalizes the labour supply chain to Thailand by the insertion of authorized labour bureaus and is bringing an increase in the share of men. Migrants are supposed to enter only via the services of an authorized bureau. The new system is declared necessary in order to make migrants safer. But since undocumented migration remains predominant, due to the costs and inflexibility of the new formal system, migrant vulnerability has actually increased and has become unsafe. The new bureaus are largely private migration- employment agencies that impose high charges and leave migrants uninformed and misinformed. Although their advance information is mostly misleading the bureaus do nothing when appealed to later by workers who are in difficulties. The high charges render most workers who use them indebted and hence insecure but tied to the agency and the assigned job. The system also has gender implications. First, prospective migrants using this channel are more dependent on parental approval and support in order to pay the charges, and so traditional gender notions often re-enter. The idea that women are more vulnerable, whereas men need a period abroad in order to grow as men, comes into play to reduce the share of women in migration. Second, domestic work is not recognized by the Lao state as an approved reason for migration; this serves as a way of asserting its honour in relation to its dominating neighbour Thailand. Women's migration into domestic work in Thailand continues as by far the largest migrant flow from Laos, given the limited domestic opportunities, but the women are forced to work irregularly in the eyes of the Lao state. Safety is not increased, while migration brokers reap gains. Policy functions contrary to its declared objectives.

Type-cast: Caste distribution of internal migrants

Majumder and Agnihotri (XXXX) in their detailed survey specifically talk about the caste aspect of internal migration in India. By investigating what are the different modes of migration (including many that diverge from the stereotype picture – circulatory; short-term seasonal; irregular short-term; medium-term; daily or weekly long-distance commuters, including urban to rural; and migration for unpaid family care) and the different types of employment, their study gives a far deeper, richer picture than do the official statistics and associated analyses. It demonstrates, for example, the concentration of migrant women workers from the scheduled castes and tribes into the most marginal, poorly-remunerated, and physically arduous employment, especially in short-term and circulatory migration and particularly for work in agriculture and brick making. In general, the current patterns of female migration do not display a major shift of migrants into new types of employment that are more 'advanced'. Instead, the relatively fast-growing and higher-status urban service occupations are largely the preserve of urban upper caste women; the women from outside the cities who enter such occupations are themselves in general of upper caste. Overall the study shows the desperate pressures on many poor women as the rural economy increasingly marginalizes some groups, groups who also have the least access to the relatively few formal sector jobs generated in the urban economy. For example, women domestic workers are usually of lower caste than the family where she is working. Majumder and Agnihotri found that among upper-caste women migrant workers the share of long-term and medium-term migration was predominant, with close to 75 per cent of them concentrated in long- and medium-term migration. In contrast, short-term and circulatory migration accounted for around 59 per cent of migrant women workers from scheduled tribes and 41 per cent of scheduled caste women migrants. The concentration of scheduled castes and tribes in this mass of general labour that circulates at the lower end of the productive economy, in which casual labour in agriculture, construction, and brick making figure prominently, draws attention to the present limitations of current migration, as conditioned by the prevailing economic and social system, in effecting the transformation of degrading feudal hierarchies.

They found Four occupations dominated the profile of the women migrant workers who responded to the individual questionnaire—agriculture (17.5 per cent), paid domestic work (15.9 per cent), brickmaking (11.8 per cent), and construction (14.3 per cent). The remaining forty per cent included vendors or petty traders, textile (spinning/tailoring/stitching) and other factory workers, home workers, sales workers in large malls as well as other shops, nurses in hospitals and other medical establishments, security guards and sanitation workers, beauticians, teachers in formal and informal educational institutions, call centre employees, a range of office workers, and professionals such as lawyers, doctors, journalists, and engineers. Apart from a well-planned policy for unorganised sectors, the migrant women worker, moving internally, needs to be taken in to mainstream of the definition of work and policy frameworks.

Finally,

Women will move and internal migration is only to rise in future with most of the migrants will be concentrating in the informal sector. So how to accept them as workers and protect their rights is a very important question, in need of an immediate policy, with a serious political will of implementing it. Otherwise the 'otherisation' and 'exclusion' of equal citizens will continue, failing the Constitutional promises of equality before law and across the Indian territory.

Reference:

Bhatt, W. (2009, February). The Gender Dimension of Migration in India: The Politics of Contemporary Space in Orissa and Rajasthan, Development in Practice, Vol. 19 No. 1.

CDRI, IDRC. (2011). Internal Migration in India: Addressing Gendered Vulnerabilities and Access to Rights : Migration, Gender and Social Justice: Connecting Research and Practice Networks, Policy Brief

No. 8

Chant, S. and Radcliffe, S.A. (1992) Migration and development: the importance of gender. In S. Chant (ed.) *Gender and migration in developing countries*. London: Belhaven Press, 1-29.

Chawla, Aruna (2015): Gender, Migration and Fundamental Rights: A Discourse on India's Commitment to its Constitution Global Research Forum on Diaspora and Transnationalism (GRFDT) Research Monograph OCTOBER

Deshingkar, Priya (2009). Circular Migration and Development in India, www.essays.ssrc.org/acrossborders/wpcontent/uploads/2009/08/ch8.pdf.

Indrani Mazumdar and Indu Agnihotri (2014): Traversing Myriad Trails: Tracking Gender and Labour Migration across India in (ed) Migration, Gender, Social Justice, and Human Insecurity, Thanh-Dam Truong, Des Gasper, Jeff Handmaker and Silver Bergh

International Labour Office (2013): Rural-urban migrants employed in domestic work: Issues and challenges: Making Decent Work a Reality for Domestic Worker in Africa: a regional knowledge sharing forum, Dar es Salaam, Tanzania, 28-30 May

Mahapatro, Sandhya Rani (2010) Patterns and Determinants of Female Migration in India: Insights from Census The Institute for Social and Economic Change, Bangalore WP 246, 2010,

MAHAPATRO, SANDHYA Rani (2015): Gender and intra-household migration decision in India: An Empirical Analysis, in Review of Social Studies (RoSS), Vol.2, No.2, Autumn

Parreñas, Rhacel S. 2001: *Servants of Globalization: Women, Migration and Domestic Work* (Stanford, CA: Stanford University Press).

Piper, N. (2008). Feminisation of Migration and the Social Dimensions of Development: The Asian Case, Third World Quarterly, Vol. 29, No. 7, Globalisation and Migration: New Issues, New Politics?, p. 1287.

Shanthi, K (2006) Female Labour Migration in India : Insights From NSSO Data MADRAS SCHOOL OF ECONOMICS, WORKING PAPER 4/2006

Thadani, V.N. and Todaro, M.P. (1984) Female migration: A Conceptual Framework. In J.T.Fawcett, S.E.Khoo and P.C.Smith *(eds.) Women in the cities of Asia*. Boulder, Colorado: Westview Press.

Truong, Thanh-Dam, Des Gasper, Jeff Handmaker and Silver Bergh (ed) (2014): Migration, Gender, Social Justice and Human Insecurity, Springer Books International, Germany

Section II

6

Photographic Studio Spaces : Representation of Women in the photographic Studios Spaces of India during the Pre-digital Era

Shreya Mukherjee

Fig 1a, A studio photograph for matrimonial purpose of Miss Durga Rani,1942 suri

"In front of the lens, I am at the same time: the one I think I am, the one I want others to think I am, the one the photographer thinks I am , and the one he makes use of to exhibit his art." Roland Barthes[1]

The confines of the photographic studio have always been an extension of our social spaces. The images they produce inside its enclosed, well-defined and controlled zones reflects the desires of the societies in which they evolved. These spaces could be for professional or personal usage but they share familiar objectives in addressing their subjects . The play between the real and the imagined - reality plays a key role in such arranged spaces. The studios with painted backdrops, selective props, controlled lights and planned proto-type postures of the sitters tend to turn into complex, spectacular spaces were the performances are staged. The visuals produced in such groomed environment echoes multiple hidden, muted meanings which have consciously been omitted from surfacing onto the well-framed, cropped visual spaces of the photographs. The photographic images, following Bárthes, can be perceived from four different angles with crossovers - what the photograph meant for the subject, how the subject wanted to portray herself/himself in front of others which depends upon what message is needed to be conveyed, the way photographer saw his subject by keeping in mind the aim and the social objective the photograph is going to serve. The fundamental objective of all studio photography tends to accomplish a goal of presenting the required, essential message through a performance which is staged in all its perfection. The equilibrium between an real and the represented desired-reality co-exist in these staged photographs.

Women were important subject to be photographed since from the advent of photography in India. 'The studio was the site for the production of the feminine images since the days of the Raj, prescribing conventions of attire, posture, and expression in portraits often delineated by women, for women. It was a space that allowed for a temporary transformation from the mundane into the spectacular'[2]. Women represented the social structure at its best in every culture. The women from different sections of society acquired their spaces in these photographic visuals, adding in making of a larger visual history. They were presented by Indian photographers in the confinement of studio spaces from as early as 1850s .The photographs during its pre-digital era portrayed women which intended for serving different reasons rather than only presenting individual personalities. The arranged spaces, seen in the photograph, into which the subjects get themselves projected were not only planned for recording but they added into making of the representation more appropriate for meeting the further required demand by its clients thus a single photographic frame have sub-layers of spatial reading which moves beyond the photograph itself. Photographic studio spaces worked as multivalent space, acting simultaneously as public and private zones. It is also depended upon the mode of circulation of the photographic images which have been captured inside these fantastic, magically controlled spaces that defines their interpretations as public, private or semi-public. The moment a image is captured it dies but gains immortality on the photographic surface to be read and re- read with the time. The photograph with time establishes their interpretative vitality and represent its time.

Tracing the works of few selected Indian photographers, the objective of this article is to understand and try to elucidate the reason behind the representation of women as a subject in the photographic studio spaces during the pre- digital era. Did the photographs portray the real women or present the women that the society wanted to see? The images of women and their representation style varied from colonial to post colonial era, as the demand of the society shifted, along with the technical advancement in photography. New social reforms for women amended with times got reflected in the photographic representation along with the fresh introduction of backdrops , props, postures and changing attire which projected the socio-cultural ambience. In photographic history women, during the colonial and pre -digital era, have constantly been portrayed as a representative of their respective societies' merits and demerits. Barring from few exceptional, they themselves, knowingly or unknowingly, becomes props in the photographs. The spaces inside the photographs and outside it compliments each other. The organizing of the space inside the studio resonates the tendencies of organizing facts which needs circulation outside it.

The 'Pardayats': women photographed within the royal courts, during the colonial era

Figure 1. Ahmed Ali Khan, Portrait of Nawaub Raj Begum Sahibah of Avadh,ca1855. British Library Board,

The three salt-print portraits, by Ahmed Ali Khan, of the royal zenana from Wajid Ali Shah's court is considered to be the earliest photographic staged representation of women in Indian context. The year was 1855.The photographs, which are in the British Library collection, London, projects a sense of a well defined, pre-arranged environment and space selection. The photographic sessions during these earliest days used to be pre-planned and workout as it involved many chemical and physical input for getting an image. Photography was an event which involves extensive processes thus it can well be assumed that the photographs of the Begums were a organized event where they could be portrayed at their best. The frames of these photographs are elaborately painted, which echoes the extension of Indian miniature tradition, is accompanied with text which compliment the images thus further completing the representation of the personalities. For instance, the inscription on fig 1 reads.

Depiction of the Deputized one, Raj Begum Sahiba, who is one of the Forbidden Ladies of His Reverence the Sultan of the World, may God render forever his rule and sultanate. But she sits outside(the women's Quarters) wearing a gold-encrusted Indian dress and her hands and ears are adorned with studded gems, a wooden gold-work diadem comb affixed upon her head, having come forth into this world of boil - and - turmoil for the purpose of depiction to meet His Reverence the Sultan of the World, may God render forever his rule and sultanate. She sits upon a silver throne at the age of twenty- three, the year 1271 of the Hijra, corresponding to the 9th year of the auspicious and(divinely) beloved enthronement. Done in the Royal Palace, Lucknow.

The inscription points out specifically the grandeur of her dress, which is Indian. It also elaborates the precious ornament with which she is adorn and refers to the silver throne she is sitting. These information along with the photographic fact emphasize on the quality of life the Begum of Wajid Ali Shah must be living. The text also states that the image has been captured inside the royal palace of Lucknow that is to establish, silently yet strongly, the strictness with which the women are confined to the private space. It is also mention in the inscription that she has come out of the women's quarter's, from behind the veil, and into this world of boil and turmoil to meet the Sultan himself.[3] These photographs were commissioned by Wajid Ali Shah. The backdrops are devoid of any decoration. They maintain a simplistic approach in contrast to the well adorned Begums.

Photography was considered capable of producing the direct truthfulness and camera was thought to be the artificial retina which captures the palpable physical evidence. 'Photography suggested that the world would become more immediate and more legible to more people than in the past.'[4] The notion of conveying the reality and thus the truth attracted many towards photography as it can serve as proof which needs to be conveyed. The representation of women through photographs, in the colonial India become a mode of disapproving the western notion of Indian inner quarters.' The zenana was widely conceived as of as a dark, damp areas of the palace, closed in and lacking fresh air. Little of the penetrating light of education was believed to find entrance, leaving the zenana a breeding ground of superstition... The inhabitants of the zenana were seen as ignorant and oppressed, idle and passive, or devious and obstinate.....'.[5] It was a constant conflict of approval and disapproval of ideas which needed support of facts thus photography became one of the best mode of presenting truth although approval of the women in presenting themselves in front of the camera is the lesser known facts.

' Many of these pejorative views of zenana were rooted in Victorian definations of sexuality. Abnormal sexual practice(such as maintaining several wives and concubines) was linked to a native ruler's 'unfitness' to govern. Polygamy was particularly abhorred as it contrasted sharply with European ideals of companionate monogamous conjugality. For these reasons, whom Indian prince chose as wives, lovers and companions was of vital concern to the colonial state, and the British actively intervened in the intimate life of the indigenous courtly family.'[6]

The photographic studio spaces during the colonial India echoed these conflicting zones. The women from the zenana were placed as evidence in front of the cameras to proof the colonial administrators, British feminist and other communities of Raj wrong. ' Photographs open up the possibilities of identity formation and performance of the subject in a changed historical context.'[7]

An account by Dr Joseph Fayrer, a British physician, who was appointed to treat one of the ill Begums of Wajid Ali Shah reveals his difficulties in treating her. He was allowed to see her after several visits later to which he was able to start his treatment. The descriptive account of Joseph Fayrer brings forth the strictness with which the inner quarters of royal, noble women were protected from the outer world. In comparison to Mr. Fayrer's account if one observe the photographs of Wajid Ali Shah's Begums, by Ahmed Ali Khan, they project an opposite account. The photographs 'records a much greater readiness to unveil, and suggest that the space in front of the camera become for many a zone for representation of selves that could not be presented elsewhere.'[8] These contradictory account related to the same zenana force us to place photography's role as a major tool for guarding the traditions of the royal courts of India. Photography never posed the threat of direct gaze thus maintaining a distance. The Camera, which worked as an artificial retina, project the neutral truth which becomes convincing proof to be presented. In these zenana portrayal by Ahmed Ali Khan bring forth the question of what urgency has given way to these photographs? Where these photographs the replacement of painting or were they presented to reveal the colonial administrator the inner quarters of the royal zenana and their well being? These images presented a legibility which might have been required during the time Wajid Ali ruled Awadh. His constant conflict with the British administrators recruited in Awadh made him walk on tight rope. Being the Nawab of Awadh he had to prove himself in front of his crowd.

Among many of his endeavors to establish his authority these photographic album leaves of his queen adds a feather in his crown by proving him as open minded King. He also legitimized the good conditions of his queen inside the 'purdha' through the photographs. The photographs were taken in closed quarters maintaining high secrecy. The zenana was a prime target for the western political audience through which they could criticize the social as well as political scenario thus overpowering the Indian royal courts. The muted threat that the royal zenana presented to the court was countered with many planned events and photography was the most immediate remedy because by not bringing the women out in the public eye the photographs in a set space represented a truth which people wanted to witness.

Presenting the royal zenana through photographs by Maharaja Sawai Ram Singh II of Jaipur similarly exemplifies his efforts to counter the then prevailing Western viewing of the Indian women quarters. Laura Weinstein finds the photography by Ram Singh II a bold modern act as these images 'broke the long standing norms of domesticity and representation'[9]. She also argues that these portraits of women and the time at which they were photographed by the Maharaja was no coincidence. These were the time when there was a keen interest in and concern towards the conditions of Indian women in *purdah* among educated Indians, colonial administrators, British feminist and other communities of the Raj. Photography as a medium were deployed to challenge the ideas central to colonialism and as far as zenana is considered the colonial idea was that the Indian women were living in a poor state of condition which needed to be rescued and reformed. In Ram Singh II 's presentation of zenana we confront an opposite image of zenana life. They are now portrayed in most' healthful and decorous specimen of feminity.'[10] Ram Singh II through his representation of the women in studio tried to convey the upgraded and self sustaining secured inner royal zenana during his rule. The women who were portrayed, quite ironically, were not the royal queens thus the notion of who should come in front of the camera was pre-decided and dictated. The painted backdrops and the props used by Sawai Ram Singh II were almost similar in all the photographs. The way they made to pose and express themselves in front of the camera and inside a controlled space, seems to be dictated by the king himself as most of the images share the similar archetypal posture and expression. The studio space of the king becomes extension of his zenana space into which his women over whom he rules acts according to his wish. Maharaja has recorded major section of women from his zenana from *pardayats* to servants. In one of the images he present a lady dressed in men's attire and poses holding a sword in her hand. A bold representational mode in comparison to its time which worked as a tool to produce images of a socially progressive life in the inner quarters of the Jaipur royal court.' By forging a new mode of representation of courtly women as decent, dignified individuals, these constitute a pictorial engagement with the wide spread discourse and a refutation of a common sentiment of the period: that women in *purdah* were idle, sexually deviant and oppressed. Paradoxically, in this defense of Rajput domestic tradition and the institution of the zenana, Ram Singh violated its most basic principle: the invisibility of its inhabitants."[11] These photographs were taken during the 1860s and 1870s. These photo- sessions took place in the photographic studio- the *Tasveer khana*- of the king himself and he was assisted by few of his attendants. The arrangement of props such as table, chair, flower vases along with the way the subject is presented within this space does not present any drastic changes giving these images a sensation of simple documentation which was aimed to serve a definite purpose. The purpose was, as assumed, meant for circulating in a close circuit of royal visitors to get a glimpse of the inner quarters of the Maharaja. The women are seen dressed in their best attire and sit upright, looking straight into the camera lens. They seems comfortable to be the part of the camera space.

The photographs by Ahmed Ali Khan and Sawai Ram Singh II represented the women from the royal court to defend the condition of zenana and its system which was complex in comparison to the western concept of family. The photographs brought the best presentation of the women, in all their perfections, from the inner women quarters of the royal household. They seem to be dressed in their best of clothes and jewelries. They serve both for family album thus private viewing but alongside these photographic set were circulated in a closed circuit to convey the staged reality from the veiled quarters of the royal. It is known that the kings had many wives and many sub-wives who controlled the zenana but few among them were given priority politically and socially thus who should be photographed was decided by the Maharaja rather than his queens.

Fig 1b. The royal couple of Tripura Maharaja Bir Chandra Manikaya and His Queen Manmohini

An unique example of women presented in the photographic space, for me, is from the royal courts of Tripura by none other than Maharaja Birchandra Manikya who got engaged in photography since mid 1860s[12] . He represented the royal ladies and his female attendants through his camera but the images seems to be much more relaxed in their representation and arrangement. Although the subjects are dressed up in proper clothes and placed in an arranged space but they seem to interact with its viewer. The fashion in which they are made to sit and look into the camera lens describes a far more elegant, artful approach. He moves far beyond the protocols of royal presentation to represent more graceful ladies with individual sensation. He was keen in photographic experimentation. He was also know for taking six poses from a single subject[13] which gives a suggestion that the King was aware of what he wanted to project in his photographs. He was a passionate practitioner of photography which gets reflected through his works. He portrayed his queens, daughters and other female attendants of his court. These photographs were meant to serve the aesthetic pleasure of the Maharaja and was not for any political usage. The poses are dictated by the Maharaja himself as he was a conscious of what he wanted to achieve. In these photographs the individual female characters gets a personality portrayal but it is the invisible presence of the King's ideas, desires and objective which can be sensed. The photography ,here, was not a medium for establishing, proving ideas through presenting visual facts but it was a medium of self expression. The role of women in these photographic spaces are more feminine and tried to remain more casual while posing.

The representation of women in photographs for public viewing

In the year 1874 a book with photographic illustrations was published and was given the title ' The Beauties of Lucknow'. This book contained a series of twenty -four albumen print portraits of courtesans from Lucknow . These have accompanying descriptive text with each. It is known from the writings of Sophie Gordon that this was published in two editions, one is in English and the other one in Urdu and was printed by Baptist mission Press in 1874. It contains a preface that states that the patrons of the volume are the gentry and nobility of Oudh. It is also stated in the volumes both edition that many of these singers, dancers and actresses were involved in production of the *'Indra- shabha'*. 'Indra -Shabha is a dramatic production popularly attributed to the lucknow based poet Agha Hasan Amanat Ali, dating 1853.[14] It is regarded as the first Urdu staged play ever written. The Indra- shabha incorporated many of the different musical, literary and dramatic styles that were current at the Awadhi court under Wajid Ali Shah. 'While the actual origin of the Indra Sabha have been debated over the years, what remained important in performances post 1857 was that the audiences believed they were beholding a direct link to the Awadhi court, which was once famous for its extravagances. This is also read as a direct connections between the story and the court of Wajid Ali Shah.'[15] It was a theatrical play enacted in Wajid Ali Shah's court during the year 1853 and after almost a gap of approximately twenty years we are witnessing the similar resonance through staged photographic images which froze within it two time frames one the imagined past of the Awadhi court and second the arranged, fantasized presentation during its own time. Post mutiny the condition the courtesans declined. They lost respect and were treated as prostitutes. These image of revert back to the past glories while holding back the reminiscence of the once rich culture of Lucknow. Each character in the photographs can be identified by their ascribed names such as Feerozah dancing girl, Lal Paree, Pearee Dancing girl, Hosenee, and others. Some of them are referred from Indra Shabha and they are dressed like paree by literary attaching feathers from their shoulders. Almost every image has the same usage of backdrop and props suggests that they were taken in the same studio space. These were meant to be seen by the elite male audience who relished the Awadhi royal court culture. The album which was meant to be seen in private. This has multiple copies which might have been bought by various clients.

2

3

4

Fig 2,3 and 4 The three images are part of twenty-four photographs from the book 'Beauties of Lucknow' by Darogha Abass Ali Khan published in 1874

Darogha Abass Ali was a municipal engineer with the colonial government in Lucknow. This was post -Mutiny time when the social conditions were disturbed and the culture was degenerating. The once respectable courtesans now been identified as singing and dancing girls. The urge to refer back to the grandeur of the Awadhi court was present among the people. It can be assumed from the publishing of this book into two languages i.e. in English and Urdu that the photographs aim to satisfy both the Indian as well as the western clients. Abbass Ali presented the women in a very dignified and graceful fashion. The backdrops remained blank with a incorporation of a heavy curtain. The props were also very selective in this arrangements- objects in regular use by the courtesans can be seen such as betel case, *hookah,* embroidered elegant hand fans with the emblem of the royal court of Awadh is represented.

5

6

Fig 5,6 The two images are part of twenty-four photographs from the book 'Beauties of Lucknow' by Darogha Abass Ali Khan published in 1874

The women are shown in most dignified way thus presenting the long lost respectable status of the courtesans from Lucknow. They seems to be confident and graceful with their best of attires and jewelries. Darogha Abbass Ali was commissioned for these photographs by those who wanted to preserve the heritage of Lucknow and simultaneously satisfy their male gaze. The setting are simple but reflects an elegance. They were also produce in the form of carte-de-visite, that is visiting card format with the images printed on them. This mean an easy circulation of image from one place to other and can be kept privately as well. These albums and their demand suggests the role women played in preserving both the cultural heritage by becoming a displayed object in these photographs thus legitimizing the imagined existence of royal past into a present which was not so comfortable a zone for these courtesans. The another known photographer contemporary to Abass Ali was Mushkoor-ud-dowlah who also captured portraits of the Lucknow courtesan.

The women, majorly, being represented in the photographs since from the advent of photography irrespective of their caste, social- status were presented to fulfill an immediate demand be it political, social, or cultural and photographic studio spaces suffice the demand to their fullest. She turns into an object of visual scrutiny. As ' in ethnographic portraits, women occupied a space of scrutiny and classification, but beyond the documentary function, they also came to be photographed for voyeuristic interest, and they were made to model as entertainers or natuch girls for postcards.'[16] The space of scrutiny and classification was occupied by the women in all the genres of photography.

A photographic studio from a small town and its representation of women

While in search for old studio photographers and photographic studios we came across Benoy Babu from Suri. His studio is located on the prime market road of Suri. It was an happening studio during 1970s and 80s. As the photography's style and demand changed the studio photography remained less popular. The introduction to digitized versions of capturing images transformed the overall visual aesthetic of photography. The studio of Benoy babu still exists but stands in its dilapidated condition. It is now run by one of his son but not anymore for studio photography purpose. He has a digital camera and a camera for shooting marriage ceremonies which is his present source of earning while Benoy Babu spends living with old memories of his photographic practice and recalls his relation with his clients. We came across old copies of his studio photographs which gave an insight to the style frame these town studios presented. People came to a studio to achieve an objective which the photograph could fulfill be it a family ,friends, self or matrimonial purpose photographs. Among other popular genres of studio photography, photographs for matrimonial purpose was in great demand. The idea which persisted behind these images were to represent the best, perfect personality reflection through a single photograph which would be circulated in appropriate places. These photographs were considered the first step towards engagement and then marriage. They were scrutinized and based on them negotiations related to marriage would start. It was surprising to see that majority of these photographs were of women only. It was the photographer who directed the best pose he thought would portray the beauty of his subject. The selection of posture and style for women would be definitely different from those of men as see in the images captured in Benoy Babus studio (refer provided images). All the photographs share the common background in which there is presence of a curtain. It is present in almost all the images. The same single chair on which the subject sits also get repeated in each photograph. The pose of the subject is well dictated by the photographer as there is repetition of posture granting the characters more feminine and dignified approach. The commonness in arrangement of space to selection of the way the characters are posed along with their gestures suggest the strong presence of the ideal conception of beauty the photographer had which he wanted to reflect through his photographs. Each photographic studio will have a trait of its own apart from a uniform approach which grants studio photography its uniqueness.

7 8

Fig 7,8 ,9 The above images are by Benoy Babu's who's studio is located in Suri,

10

11

12

Fig 10, 11, 12 The above images are by Benoy Babu's who's studio is located in Suri,

13

14

Fig 13,14 The above images are by Benoy Babu's who's studio is located in Suri,

Studio spaces for photography defined a social ideas about the women. The representation of women in these indoor spaces re-define the role they played to express the social demand . These photographs reveals the stories and parallel historical evidences which supports to untangled the cultural reading. Studio spaces reflected the inner stories of the spaces the women marked in our societies.

Image Acknowledgement:

- The image in Fig 1 is from the book 'Afterimage of Empire-photography in Nineteenth-century India'- Zahid R.Chaudhary. The collection is in British Library London.
- The images in Fig 1b, 2,3,4,5,6 are from Wikimedia Commons
- The images from Fig 1a, 7,8,9,10,11,12,13,14 and 1a are from authors collection.

Endnotes

1 Barthes, Roland, Camera Lucida: Reflection on Photography, Translated by Richard Howard, 1981,pg 13.

2 Narain, Suryanandini, Photographing the Feminine, Framing women: Gender in the colonial Archive, Marg Vol. 62, No.4,2011, pg 34.

3 Choudhary, Zahid.R, "Armor and Aesthesis", In Afterimage of Empire-Photography in the 19th century India, pg 31.

4 Warien, Mary Warner, Photography and Its Critis, A cultural History 1839-1900, Cambridge University Press, 1997,2007.

5 Weinstein, Lura. Exposing the zenana: Maharaja Sawai Ram Sing II's photographs of Women in Purdah, History of Photography, Routledge 2010, pg 6.

6 Jhala,Angma Dey, Royal Patronage, power and Aesthetic in Princely India, Routledge, London and New York, 2011, pg 109-110.

7 Banerjee, Debalina. Boundaries of the self : Gender,culture and spaces, pg103.

8 Pinney, Christopher. Camera work as technical practice in colonial India,

9 Weinstein, Lura. Exposing the zenana: Maharaja Sawai Ram Sing II's photographs of Women in Purdah, History of Photography, Routledge 2010, pg2-16.

10 Ibid.pg 8.

11 Ibid, pg 3.

12 Ghosh, Siddharta, Chobi-tola, Bangalir photographic chorcha. Ananda publishers 1988, pg 26.

13 Karlekar, Malavika. Re-vision the past-Early photography in Bengal 1875- 1915, Oxford University Press, New York.2005,pg 149.

14 Gordon, Sophie. Monumental Vision: Architectural Photography in India- 1840-1901, Phd. Thesis.SOSA,2011,pg194.

15 Ibid,pg194

16 Sinha, Suryanandini, Facing the Lens- Women in Bombay's Photographic Studio's, from The Artful pose- Early studio Photography in Mumbai 1855-1940, Dr. Bhau Daji Lad Museum City Mumbai, Alkazi Collection of Photography, Mapin Publishing,2010.pg 45.

7

The Story of *Kironmala* from *Thakurmar Jhuli*–Feisty Bengali Princess Breaking Norms

Lopamudra Maitra Bajpai

Folktales have their own interpretation as they mark a special socio-cultural ethos of various culture. From the genre of oral traditions as the stories travel down the course of history to the modern age of popular culture, the stories experience a changeover in terms of portrayal of representations and their pattern of storytelling. This paper looks into a specific folktale- *Kironmala*- from Bengal (undivided Bengal and before the Indian independence-followed by the partition of 1947- encompassing the present state of West Bengal in India and the neighbouring country of Bangladesh). The otherwise well-known folktale features amidst the collection of *Thakurmar Jhuli* (Grandmother's Bag of Tales) - which is a most popular collection first published by under the efforts of Dakkhinaranjan Mitra Majumdar in 1907. Marking a distinct voice of the lead character in *Kironmala*- the storyline highlights a young woman-performing 'heroic' acts of bravery and valour- which otherwise used to be accorded to be parts of the 'heroic deeds of men'. *Kironmala* attempts to break away from the patriarchal mould- even while distinctly trying to maintain its ethos of the 'portrayal of a good and homely woman'.

This paper looks into the original folktale and its format from the book- *Thakurmar Jhuli-* that represents a well-charted gender-based ideation quite similar in lines to most folktales around the world. Across the last couple of years- the story of *Kironmala* has also been adapted across several platforms of popular culture as popular Bengali television serials. The paper attempts to highlight a 'voice'- breaking away from the standard pattern and evolving to create a niche for representing itself amidst a global world through the world of popular culture. The story of the brave princess- *Kironmala* was also highlighted by the author at the 3rd IAAH Conference, Sri Lanka – 2015 (International Association for Asian Heritage) held at the University of Kelaniya[1].

Kironmala- Women, Folklore and Popular Culture

March 2015 marked a gala event in the city of Kolkata to announce the beginninga television serial based on the story of *Kironmala*. The serial ran through nearly two years- till the last episode was aired in November 2016. Amidst much fanfare and popularity, the fairytale story of *Kironmala* survived to witness a popularity of folktales through the effective medium of popular culture. This venture to televise (albeit transformed and rescripted) version of the folktale- *Kironmala* albeit had its share of 'cinematic representation of drama', nevertheless the story maintained the flow of the fearless and feisty princess- moving out to save the world and her kingdom.

The original story of *Kironmala*speaks of a brave princess, who saves her family and kingdom against all evil. As it forms an important part of*Thakurmar Jhuli*- the original compilation by Bengali author- Dakkhina ranjan Mitra Majumdar. The book (available in English translations as well) still stands as an outstanding example from Bengal to highlight one of the oldest attempts by an Indian to collect, compile and publish folktales collected regionally.[2]

Mostly collected from the district of Mymensingh of the present country of Bangladesh[3], the efforts of Majumdar might not seem unique today in comparison to present range of publications available across the nation however, more than a hundred years back, the effort was unique and genuine in a manner that it was not a scholarly attempt for the erudite community, but an uncomplicated endeavour to retain a sense of originality about the basic tenets of life- folkstories- which carry an important socio-cultural ethos and essence of a region. The attempt was to maintain and preserve a cultural pattern- especially preserved for posterity.[4] Though, often criticised to have been limited to the mere intellectual and erudite urban crowd of the undivided region of Bengal (including the present country of Bangladesh and the state of West Bengal in India)- this also brings into focus the important debate about the transcription of folktales and lore on one side as well as the bigger picture of representation on the other. With reference to representations, an important focus of the present paper is the construction of the identity of gender and women's identities and attempts of de-constructing specific notions. Oral traditions come in as an important tool with reference to the creation of such identities as "the hierarchical relations between the two sexes are not accidental, but the result of an acculturation process. This disparity is culturally maintains, learned and internalised in practice both through cultural concepts and disperse, verbal and non-verbal." (Lalita Handoo:145). With oral traditions bearing the responsibilities of 'labelling roles and duties' as well- the transcription of the same lore into various versions of publication as well as broadcast ideas also bears special significance. "Language, being a product of culture and the only means of verbal communication, not only reflects the socio-cultural structure of the society, but also reinforces its ideological practices in various ways. This also happens to be the most powerful tool for control and transmission of knowledge, culture and otherwise."

(*Ibid*). On the path of creating identities through a codified and transcripted procedure as the various publications of oral traditions and folktales give a specific 'concrete shape and structure' to the many gender-symbols- it also takes into consideration the important part of the acceptance of specific terms, symbols and concepts by the society at large and in turn such representations also further builds up an 'image' of the genders and their roles within our patriarchal set-ups as"...concept formation is a cultural activity shared by the entire group, and precedes language codification and lexicalisation. Languages all the time make use of their available devices to lexicalise these concepts to reinforce the socio-cultural values and ideologies. These values not only determine the attitudes of a group but also have direct bearing on the lexicalisation process of the language and the language behaviour of its speakers." (*Ibid*). Keeping in line with the general story pattern ofmost folktales from across the globe, all the tales of *Thakurmar Jhuli* highlights the commonly expressed notions and stereotypes as is commonly associated with the female gender. Also- following the pattern- these stereotypes and gender biases act as powerful tools to reinforce the cultural values that is commonly and easily accepted. Thus, more often than not the various stories describe the many women characters as quarrelsome, untrustworthy, unintelligent, belligerent, evil and most of them are shown to not have any contribution with social gatherings, especially in the presence of her husband. The gender stereotypes within the stories are also reflected through a common theme of abandonment, isolation and abduction. As clear shows of power-displays dominate and re-establish the gender roles within these stories amidst our patriarchal moulds- they also further help to stereotype the role of the 'unwanted wife'- who is severely punished at several instances by being banished within the forest. More often than not- these stories of abandonment and banishment also reminds one of the famous Indian epic- *The Ramayana*- where the female protagonist suffers the same fate in a condition of pregnancy and is banished to the forest. Sita's husband- the king of Ayodhya was Rama and he had to banish the queen on alleged allegations by his countrymen questioning the chastity of Sita as she was previously abducted by the Asura king Ravana and a long battle ensued between Rama and Ravana to rescue Sita. Though Ravana was slayed and Sita was rescued without any harm, but an accusation followed her about her honourable nature and chastity for her long period as a captive under Ravana. Being plagued by the same question time and again, Rama chose to be an ideal role-model as a king for his subjects and finally had to banish Sita to the forests. *The Ramayana* forms an important part of the mainstream/greater tradition of Indian lore and it is not surprising to have left its various influences across a multitude of lores from across the nation. The influence may have also worked the other way- with the various folklore from across the nation influencing to form give rise to a single story that came to be popular all over. The role and significance of this influence is yet to be ascertained and can form a significant part of a study in years to come.Coming back to the present discussion of the storyline, it is understood thus, that the many stories of *Thakurmar Jhuli* which speaks of a specific king banishing his wife- could have been heavily influenced by the story of *The Ramayana*. Highlighting similarities and stereotypes- it is also important to mention the story of *Kironmala* to begin with a similar concept- with several wicked women creating a lie- leading to the banishment of the queen to the forest by the king in sheer agony and anger. However, it is the later part of the story which concerns the paper- as the storyline evolves into a prominent character to portray a female through an unusual light. The paper further attempts to look at the same through the recent attempts of inclusion of the story within popular culture of the broadcast media as a popular television serial in Bengali language. The high TRP (Television Rating Point) chart of the specific show- *Kironmala*-helped it to sustain itself across two years of broadcast- the rewriting of the story adapted for television also entailed into changing the structure as well as the components of the original folktale published in *Thakurmar Jhuli*. However- across the new adaptation or the original one- the underlined essence remains as the central focus- speaking of a courageous princess- who braves all evil to save her family and kingdom.

As the Story Evolves – From *Thakurmar Jhuli* to Modern Global Broadcast Media

According to the original story published in *Thakurmar Jhuli- Kironmala* is a folktale of three royal children- *Arun, Barun and Kironmala*- who were orphaned and abandoned at birth by their jealous maternal- aunts who were supervising the delivery of their mother. The aunts put them in clay pots andfloat them down a nearby river in an attempt to kill them. The infants were replaced by a puppy, a kitten and a wooden doll across three consecutive deliveries. All these three replacements were also shown to the father- the king. The latter- dismayed about the fact that the queen is unable to produce 'human babies' – banished the unfortunate queen from the kingdom. On the other hand, the abandoned infants- born across three years- floated down the river and reached a pious and childless Brahmin priest- who brought them up like his own. After sometime, when the children were young adolescents, the priest passed away- leaving his all to the three kids. The young children began to redecorate and rebuilt their old and worn-down home. This remodelling took a wonderful shape and attracted the attention one day of a passing-by priest. Struck by the wonderous construction, this priest advised them to redecorate their home with magical birds, trees and flowers from a magical land afar. Tempted, the brothers proceeded one after the other to get the jewels form the magical land. However, time passed and neither of the brothers returned.*Kironmala* finally donned the attire of a prince with a sword and went to rescue her brothers. One the way, as several evil creatures attempted to devour her and tempt her away from her path, *Kironmala* remained steadfast and finally managed to rescue her brother, along with several other princes who were all cursed earlier and turned into stones and mountains. Thus- all three siblings returned with the magical, talking birds and invited the king over for a luncheon. As the bemused king sat down for a feast, the magical bird revealed a folly committed by the king many years ago- reminding him about the impossible scenario of "a human being giving birth to a puppy, a kitten and a wooden doll." Thus, revealing the true identity of the three siblings, the magical bird helped to unite the children with their father. The mother who was living a desolate and lonely life across a riverbank was also united by the magical bird- and all the members of the family returned home contented and they all lived happily ever after.

Thus as the main storyline follows in the published adaptation, the many screenplays across the last couple of decades however- had their own adaptations. Such a screenplay was created for the 1st time for an on-screen full-length feature film in Bengali in 1979 (language- Bengali, Genre- Fantasy). The name of this film was-*Arun BarunKironmala-* had a slightly different portrayal of the structure of the folktale. The film portrayed the three siblings- Arun, Barun and Kironmala as orphaned brothers and sisters at birth. One day they went in search of their parents and landed in the court of a female magician- the *Jogini Durbar-* where they were helped with magical equipments like a golden stick etc. Then they went to an enchanted land- *Maya Puri-* where they found spirits and fairies trapped by the witch of the *Maya Puri*. After many hurdles they finally killed the witch and helped the fairies to escape. The fairies then promised to tell them about their parents. They were taken for lunch to the *Jogini Durbar* where the king of Arabia also joined them. It was soon discovered that the three children were the children of this king. The five fairies revealed how the sister of the king's wife played tricks and let the three children float down the river for which the king punished his wife and banished her from the palace forever. Finally there was a happy reunion and Arun, Barun & Kironmala found their parents and all lived happily ever after.

Three and a half decades later, another screenplay adapted the same story- of course with its own variations- which is the serial of *Kironmala* as mentioned in the beginning of this paper. This- being the latest adaptation of the original folktale- started as a lengthy television serial (from August 2015) highlighting the struggles of a lone princess- *Kironmala*- who battles an evil queen and her equally evil compatriots to save her kingdom- *Achinpur* from destruction. Glitzy clothes and makeup and computerised set design and backdrop made up for all the visual depictions needed to make a fairytale come to life in stark contradiction to the lengthy story in its original format.

From oral traditions to publications to the modern genre of popular culture- as adaptations changed with audience preferences across time, the story of *Kironmala* has been reincarnated each time as a new *avatar*. However, as the components changes within a tale from oral tradition, the structure represents a continuity of representing the central character- a princess as a courageous braveheart who shouldered the great responsibility of saving her family and thereby her kingdom and finally reuniting with her family. However, an analysis of this representation will not be complete until an assessment of the storyline of all other stories of *Thakurmar Jhuli* is complete. The original storyline of *Kironmala* from *Thakurmar Jhuli* narrates a story of an 'otherwise homely girl, who transforms into a braveheart by embodying all the significant features of a warrior prince'. This is effectively portrayed through the portrayal of attitude, clothes and appearance of the young princess. In order to 'turn into a braveheart', she is described to don the clothes of a prince as well as carry a sword and wear a turban/head gear like a prince. She is also portrayed as a female who does not have any'greed' towards 'jewels and precious stones' being a 'rural maiden' with 'simple tastes' and thus is never 'tempted by evil forces' when sheventured out to save her brothers. Her brothers, quite unlike her, had 'yielded to the evil temptations of precious and semi-precious stones and jewels' and were thus cursed and turned into stones in a mountain. This mountain contained several other cursed princes's who were all 'tempted by evil forces and being males' yielded to their passion- ultimately leading to a curse. However, *Kironmala* braved all temptations and finally managed to save all men in the story and reunite her siblings with their father- the king. Across her description in her life as a 'homely girl' under the Brahmin priest, *Kironmala* is variously described as a 'dutiful daughter who keeps the house pristine clean, feeds the cows in the cowshed, waters the plants, cooks wonderful meals, as her brothers study to become erudite scholars.' Even after returning, as she 'helps her brothers to redecorate their abode, she quickly rechanges into the garb of a dutiful daughter.'

The storyline of the movie, with its slight variations, shows the lead character being helped at various places by her siblings and though she remains central to the idea, yet is shown to be at par with her brothers. Finally, in the story of the television serial, *Kironmala* is shown as the lonely princes, who struggles and fights against all odds to save all people connected to her life, including her lover. Thus, needless to say, as adaptations evolved with newer ideas, roles of women, accorded within the storyline also evolved with time.

To understand the evolution of the parallel themes within the main storyline of *Kironmala*- it is important to understand certain accepted norms about folklore. Following the pattern of all oral traditions, the story of *Kironmala* also is a reflective of oral traditions from Bengal (undivided and pre- 1947) and as is the generally accepted notion about folklore- it also survives within a particular society because it fulfils certain social functions which can be many and also, on the other hand, be specific to certain cultures. These can be broadly grouped into (Bhattacharya D.K., 2005)[5]—

- Recreation or amusement
- Education
- Socialization
- Protest or propaganda
- Communication of knowledge

Following the patriarchal representation, similar to other stories within *Thakurmar Jhuli*- the centuries-old original publication of the book- speak of portraying all of the above. An underlined essence of subjugation of women took the centreplace and ran across all folkstories from Bengal- quite like the gender stereotypes spoken earlier. Several stories across medieval and modern Bengal affirm the same- with a stringent class and caste divided society- imposing conservative and strict rules on the behaviour and roles of women in the society. With few sections of urban elite experiencing a so-called renaissance of sorts especially in cities like Kolkata, a major part of the rural population remained away from the basic touches of women's emancipation for many decades. Their social roles were reduced to mere homemakers, mothers and more often than not, their significance were weighted upon the many number of male child each could bear. Limiting all roles of women within the paradigms of the household alone, all the oral traditions, including the ones within *Thakurmar Jhuli*- evolved across the last thousand years to speak of a secondary role of a woman, heavily guarded by the patriarch and often punished according to the whims and fancies of the dominant gender.Emphasising upon rural lifestyles of allocating roles towards specific genders, these stories encoded the same gendered messages which the first television advertisements and serials did in the early 1950s across USA. Setting up specific gender roles within a community, these stories thus respecified times and spaces and the primary and secondary characters within a society and a culture. The secondary roles of women thus, in *Thakurmar Jhuli-* oscillates between being an evil character on one side or being a pitiable one who has been abandoned, banished orsubjected to immense misery, until an important man in their lives- e.g. their husbands or sons would finally come and rescue them from their tragedy. Amidst this portrayal of the stories of *Thakurmar Jhuli-* thus- the story of *Kironmala* stands apart. She is a voice amidst the patriarchal set-up- who refuses to follow the norms. This however doesn't allow her to completely discard her 'lady-like features and characteristics', but she is given enough freedom to 'transform' into a braveheart. Thus, *Kironmala* only adorns the clothes of a warrior to save the two princeses. Throughout the course of her action in the pursuit of her brothers- she is hardly given any dialogues and continues to perform her work 'silently'. This more often than not transforms the brave princess to a mere helper- as the sphere of her action is different from what the male dominated society has otherwise assigned her to do. The patriarchal value system is once again affirmed through the lack of dialogue, 'silently helping other' and the portrayal of the fact that *Kironmala* immediately returns to her 'usual' lifestyle upon returning home and continues to tend to domestic chores. References of this across folklore is not uncommon the world over and with respect to the storyline of *Kironmala-* one can easily recognise specific symbols which also corresponds to the language and gender theory of Robin Lakoff (1973- Language and Women's Place[6]). *Kironmala*'s story especially signifies the use of politeness (extreme display while speaking), expression of emotion (extreme emotional exaggeration is displayed), extended vocabulary (long and descriptive languages to describe the woman and her surroundings and her activities), lack of humour (the women is hardly referred to express any humour). However, some of the obvious symbols, e.g. extreme use of politeness, lack of humour, expression of exaggerated emotion- are traits which seems to have diminished in their representation across the several broadcast adaptations in later years. With changing times, the newer adaptations reflect a different approach. Keeping the basic structure, the components within is altered to suit the likes and tastes of modern global audiences. Also- the basic shift from print publication to audio-visual broadcast media also demands the natural inclusion and deletion of specific symbols of expression- e.g. extended vocabulary, exaggerated emotion, etc- are taken care of by the script, screenplay and computer graphics. Thus, moving from the domain of oral traditions to print publications and finally audio-visual broadcast media- the story of *Kironmala*evolved to break away from the stereotype and create a mark of its own- which inspired all the modern renditions to speak of a liberated woman and her fight for justice and truth.

Conclusion

It is important to understand the basic underlying essence of socio-cultural representative patterns across all stories of *Thakurmar Jhuli*. A.K. Ramanujan (*Folktales from India*, 1985) classified folktales undervarious plots, such as chain tales, ritual tales, trickster tales, or sibling tales. Quite distinctly, yet maintaining a simple representation of facts for the young audience, the collection in *Thakurmar Jhuli* is also classified into four distinct categories: Tales of adventure (*Dudher Sagar*), Tales of demons (*Roop Tarashi*), Animal and Humorous tales (*Chang Bang*), and poems explaining the ritual of putting the children to sleep at the end of the stories (*Aam Sandesh*). The present story- *Kironmala*- is a part of the first section which has six stories- *Roop Tarashi* (Tales of Adventure). [7]

. It is the 6th story of sub-section and stands quite distinctly apart from the rest in its representation of the lead character- a young female.Maranda and Maranda describes folklore communication as narratives, serving the function of informationtransmission where the storyteller acts as an encoder and the codesas symbols, which are constructed out of the cultural mosaic, and thelisteners as the decoders. Thus, it should also be kept in mind that, thecodes and symbols used in one context may not be relevant to anothercontext. However, the elucidation and involvement of codes and symbolsis an intrinsic tool for the analysis of folklore. Whether these symbols areculture specific or can transgress cultures is also another genre that needsto be analysed. On the other hand, certain symbols can be developed toact as specific discourses between cultures. As D.K. Bhattacharya rightlypoints out (2005), the ethnic mind rightly chooses its own positive andnegative scale of references in order to constantly map the path betweenthe 'We' and the 'They' in their cognition. Thus, age-old stories of *Thakurmar Jhuli*take a new meaning for young minds everytime any or all of the stories are rescripted onto New Media,

Resembling all other stories from the compilation of *Thakurmar Jhuli*- the story of *Kironmala* too reflects a specific cognitive pattern. Oral traditions have always been one of the simplest of mediums through which thevillage women's (in this case the women of Bengal- under the torment of domestic life, heavy burden of taxes, penury condition with poverty, famine, drought and floods – forming a regular part of most rural lifestyle across the last thousand years of Bengal's history) dreams of becoming queens, princesses or to be off onadventures '*across seven seas and thirteen rivers*' (an aspect often reflected though most of the stories of *Thakurmar Jhuli*) could literally cometrue; in the realm of fantasy. Likewise, these were also cautionary talesthat preached submission and docility in women, though, some of them[8] also oppose this common-held notion and the tales reflect that in thestories of *Kironmala*. In *Kironmala*thus, the boldand fearless princess goes in search of her brothers and otherprinces, on a mission where all men have failed and she fights all evil towin at the end. The common strand that continues through all the cautionarytalesis- that they teach women to be passive (justified by the use and display of specific languages as mentioned earlier), nevertheless, bold enoughto take responsibility for their lives and act, defying words of caution and toface any situation if need be[9]. Nevertheless, the story also often maintains the general rhythm of stereotypical exaggerated emotion with respect to women- which can best be summarised in the final verses of the story through a poem- expressing the woe of a childless woman or a person who has lost her child at birth (refer to the exaggerated display of emotion through the chhara/poem)-

"Shonar pakhi gaan korilo,-
"Arun, Barun, Kiron,
Teen bhuboner teen dhon.
Emon roton hariye, chhilo
Michhai jibon.
Arun Barun Kironmala
Aaj ghuchali shokol jala"
(Translation-
The magical golden bird started singing
Arun, Barun, Kiron,
The three jewels from heaven, earth and sky,
I do not know how I survived by losing you.
Arun, Barun, Kironmala
I am the happiest today after reuniting with you)

Drawing to a close with the words for happily ever after, *Kironmala*'s story comes to a happy ending as well. With later adaptations remoulding the basic storyline, the central character however continues to highlight a steadfast and courageous woman- who went out to save the world and thus, her bravery is immortalised, inspite of all patriarchal representations as sub-texts within the same storyline. The folktale remains a lone example from more than a century old compilation of *Thakurmar Jhuli* which spoke of breaking away from stereotypes and finding a voice within the niche space of limited representation.

Figures-

Fig.1- The first picture at the beginning of the story showing the clay pot with the abandoned children floating down the river and reaching the Brahmin priest as he performs his early morning ablutions in the river

(pp. 95. Note the elaborate garb of the Brahmin priest performing his puja- marked by details including the *gamchha*[10] on the shoulder and the sacred thread across the shoulder- referred to in Bengali as *poitey*. The depiction is to reconfirm the 'pious and sacrosanct' upbringing of the three abandoned siblings)

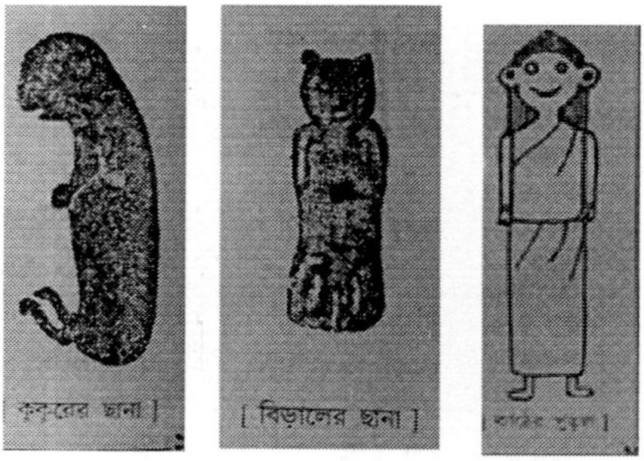

Fig. 2- The three consecutive births of the three children were replaced by the evil aunts with a puppy, a kitten and a wooden toy female doll respectively.

(pp. 98-99. Note the detailing to describe the two young ones of dog and cat respectively. The wooden doll is a traditional item of handicraft from Bengal and still stands as an important ethnic item which are purchased by people far and wide)

Fig.3- The three siblings sees the king (their father) for the first time- close to their hut in the forest

(pp. 104. Note- the pristine garb of the siblings to denote a sacrosanct upbringing by the Brahmin priest- including the sacred thread on the shoulders of the brothers/*poitey* and the simple hut in the background)

Fig. 4- The wise ascetic who informs the three siblings about the mountain of precious stones

(pp. 106. Note the palace that the three siblings has built in the background)

Fig. 5- Kironmala venturing out to save her brothers with hands on the hilt of her sword

(pp. 109. Note- the various animals as well as demons painted around the protagonist and she is seen in a typical garb of the Islamic rulers/nawabs of Bengal form medieval times.

Fig. 6- Kironmala makes all the stones come back to life by sprinkling magical water from the golden pot

(pp.112. Note- the detailed garb of the princess- *Kironmala*- including the headgear- resembling the attire of the Islamic nawabs/kings of Bengal in medieval times

Fig.7- The king sitting down for his lunch being invited by the three siblings when the magical bird reminded him of his folly from many years ago.

(pp. 115. Note the difference in clothing between the siblings as the feisty Kironmala returns back to her domestic duties and is seen adorning the usual garb of a common / lay man, while her brothers are seen wearing the clothes befitting a king- including the headgear. Also- Kironmala assumes charge of all domestic chores and is seen cooking and serving the guest/king)

Fig.8- The poster of the movie (1979) *Arun Barun Kironmala*- showing the new additional character to the story- the witch of Mayapuri[11]

Fig. 9- The poster of the television serial (2015) *Kironmala*- showing the new additional character to the story- the loyal boyfriend of the princess who helps her in her tedious path[12]

References

Bhattacharya, Ashutosh, 1927. *Banglar Lok Samskriti* (Bengali). National Book Trust, New Delhi, India.

Bhattacharya, D.K., 2005. *Studying folklore—The Indian Experience*. Lecture paper unpublished, University of Delhi, India. Bhattacharya, D.K., 2006. The Development Dilemma in Tribal India. Lecture paper unpublished, Paper presented as Special Lecture in the Session on Anthropology, Indian Science Congress, Hyderabad, India.

Blackburn, Stuart H. and A.K. Ramanujan, (ed.) 1986. *Another Harmony: New Essays on the Folklore of India*. Oxford University Press, New Delhi, India. Dawson Infotech, 2005:

Handoo, Lalita 2006*The Discourse of Gender: Power and Practice*. In M.D. Muthukumaraswamy (ed.) Folklore as Discourse. Chennai: National Folklore Support Centre

http://www.dawsen.com Dawsen Infotech's adaptation ofDakkhinaranjan Mitra Majumdar's, *Thakurmar Jhuli*, 2006. (Bengali), Dawsen Infotech, Kolkata, India.

Jaya Bhattacharji 2006*Folklore and Children's Literature*. In Indian Folklife- a quarterly newsletter from National Folklore Support Centre,Serial No. 21, (April 2006). Chennai, India.

Kailash C. Baral 2006*Globalisation and Tribes of Northeast India*. In Indian Folklife- a quarterly newsletter from National Folklore Support Centre, Serial No. 22,(July 2006). Chennai, India.

Kironmala movie, 1979. Director- Barun Kabasi, Dolphin Films. Kolkata, India.

Kironmala television serial 2015. Director-Indradeep Dasgupta. Surinder Films.

Lakoff, Robin 1973 *Language and Women's Place*. In Language in Society, Vol. 2, No. 1 (Apr. 1973). pp. 45-80. Harper and Row: New York:

Maitra (Bajpai), Lopamudra 2013. *Indian Folk Lore and the Three Worlds of Experiences: A New Theory to Understand 'Learning' from Folk Lore in Modern Audio Visual Media for Children*. In Mrinmoy Pramanick, Md. Intaj Ali, ed. Indian Journal of Comparative Literature and Translation Studies, Volume 1, Number 1, September, 2013. University of Hyderabad: India.

- 2013. *Stories of Tuntuni from Bengal- Connecting Oral Traditions with the Global Age Across a Century*. In In Heritage and Us (English e-journal) – Year 2, Issue-1, March/April 2013 http://go.epublish4me.com/ebook/ebook?id=10023475

- 2012. *Oral-written nexus in Bengali Chharas over the last hundred years: Creating new paradigm for children's literature*. In Journal SAARC CULTURE- Vol 3- 2012- 15 SAARC Culture Centre, Colombo, Sri Lanka, 2012

- 2012. *Mednipur patachitra from West Bengal (India)- Folk art re-invented through modern media and communication* (Sri Lanka). In Asian Art and Culture- A research volume in Honour of Ananda Coomaraswamy. Sri Lanka: Centre for Asian Studies, University of Kelaniya, 2012

- 2011. *Bengali graphic novels for children-Sustaining an intangible heritage of storytelling traditions from oral to contemporary literature* (India). In Folklore and Folkloristics (English e-journal) – Vol. 4, No. 2. (December 2011)-

http://www.google.co.in/url?sa=t&rct=j&q=&esrc=s&frm=1&source=web&cd=1&ve d=0CCsQFjAA&url= http%3A%2F%2Fwww.indianfolklore.org%2Fjournals%2Findex.php%2Ffofolk%2Farticle%2 Fdownload% 2F1159%2F1368&ei=8BLIUeHJNorsrAeViYGQAw&usg=AFQjCNGlFt_md7D8pc1spOZJUF0WZy SEZQ&sig2=uAIlMZOR d0CrUP4slJo0Ng

- 2011. *Oral traditions reaching beyond peripheries in modern era of mass communication- A case study of Radh region of West Bengal* (India). In LOUKIK (bilingual journal in English and Bengali) – Volume-4, Issue No. 1 & 2, 2011. Kolkata.

- 2010. *Communicating words and more:- A study of oral traditions of Radh Bengal (including the districts of Purulia, West Mednipur and Bankura)*. In IFRJ- Indian Folklore Research Journal- Issue No. 10, December 2010. Chennai.

- 2008. *Childrens' oral literature and modern mass media in India with special reference to gradual transformation in West Bengal.* In IFRJ- Indian Folklore Research Journal- Vol 5, Number-8, 2008. Chennai.

- 2007. *100 years of Thakurmar Jhuli (Grandmother's Bag of Tales)-From Oral Literature to Digital Media-Shaping Thoughts for the Young and Old.* In IFRJ- Indian Folklore Research Journal- Issue-7, 2007. Chennai.

Mitra, Bansari, 2002. The Renovation of Folk Tales by Five Modern Bengali Writers, Anthropological Survey of India, Kolkata, India.

Majumdar, Dakkhinaranjan Mitra, 1907. Thakurmar Jhuli (Bengali). Mitra and Ghosh Publisher Pvt. Ltd, Kolkata, India.

Majumdar, Dakkhinaranjan Mitra, 2007. Thakurmar Jhuli (Bengali) comic book. Rajendra Library, Kolkata, India.

Propp, Vladimir, 1958. Morphology of the Folktale. Volume 9 of the Bibliographical and Special Series of the American Folklore Society, Indiana University Research Centre in Anthropology, Folklore and Linguistics, Bloomington, Indiana, USA.

Rantanen, Terhi, 2005. The Media and Globalisation. Sage Publications Ltd, UK.

Roychowdhury, Proshit, 2007. October 28: Thakurmar Jhulir Eksho Bochchor. Bartoman Newspaper Sunday. Bartoman Papers, Kolkata, West Bengal, India.

Sadhana Naithani, "Folklore and Media." Indian Folklife–a quarterly newsletter from National Folklore Support Centre, Vol 4, Issue 1 Serial No. 18, (January 2005). Chennai, India.

http://archive.thedailystar.net/lifestyle/2010/03/05/page02.htm

http://www.museindia.com/viewarticle.asp?myr=2011&issid=38&id=2707

Endnotes

1 http://repository.kln.ac.lk/bitstream/handle/123456789/11515/4.pdf?sequence=1&isAllowed=y. The 3rd IAAH Conference, Sri Lanka – 2015- Author- self

2 Maitra (Bajpai) 2007 *100 years of Thakurmar Jhuli.* pp- 79-80. In Indian Folklore Research Journal, Vol.4, No.7, 2007: 77-95 © 2007 National Folklore Support Centre

3 Under undivided and pre 1947 India, the district of Mymensingh formed an integral part of the state of West Bengal in India

4 *Ibid* pp 80

5 *Ibid* pp- 81

6 Robin Lakoff- from Language in Society. Vol 2, No.1 (Apr. 1973), pp. 45-80

7 *Ibid*

8 *Ibid*83

9 *Ibid* 84

10 *Gamchha*- literally a hand-woven piece of cloth used as a towel- but much thinner than its western counterparts. Often it is also used to cover the head or the upper part of the body while performing puja as per the requirements. The picture from *Kironmala* portrays such an example.

11 https://en.wikipedia.org/wiki/Arun_Barun_O_Kiranmala#/media/File:Arun_Barun_O_Kiranmala.jpg- poster of the 1979 Bengali film- *Arun Barun Kironmala*

12 http://www.hotstar.com/tv/kiranmala/1676- poster of the 2015 Bengali television serial *Kironmala*

8

'Cultural Space' in Women's Travel Writings: A Comparative Study Between Two Bengali Travelogues

Md. Iqbal Sultan

Introduction

James Clifford views travel as a translation term for comparative cultural studies whereby the blurring between dwelling and travelling is revealed, and "constructed and disputed historicities, sites of displacement, interference and interaction, come more sharply into view" (James Clifford, 1992). Clifford proposes the use of 'travel' in cultural comparison— "... precisely because of its historical taintedness, its associations with gendered, social bodies, class privilege, specific means of conveyance, beaten paths, agents, frontiers, documents and the like. I prefer it to more apparently neutral, and 'theoretical' terms, such as 'displacement' which can make the drawing equivalence across different historical experiences to easy" (Clifford 1992 : 110).

Both travel and travel writing are hermeneutic processes whereby the 'eye/I' of the traveller/travel writer constructs spatial and textual difference (Alison Mary Blunt 1992:32). Travel writing is distinctive because autobiographical narrative exists alongside, and seems to gain authority from observational detail. The journey undertaken and represented can be seen as a psychological journey, relating to themes of the journey of life and self-discovery. Such self-referentiality parallels that of diary narratives because—"... in much the same way as the diarist assesses public or cultural codes to mitigate the split between narrating self and narrated self, he or she can also fall back on and analogy between a geographical journey and spiritual journey : the traveller can view the journey as destined towards a place in which narrator and actor are reconciled, in a visionary self-presence" (Louis A. Renza, 1980).

In the present study two Bengali travelogues on foreign countries have been taken into account. The first one is 'Bangomohilar Japan Yatra'(1915) by Hariprava Takeda and the second one is 'Farasi Desh Anyo Chokhey' (1998) by Priti Sanyal. Probably in Bengali, 'Bangomohilar Japan Yatra' was the first travelogue on Japan. Being a mere housewife, Smt. Takeda has given a complete picture of society and culture of Japan at that time. On the contrary, Priti Sanyal dwelled in France for near about two decades. She had the chance of observing the country very closely. The author vividly described socio-cultural issues, racial problems and expansion of Indian Culture in France. The outlook of the authors is different but both of them depicted the 'Cultural Space' of the respective regions which is significant in respect of Cultural Geography.

Objectives

i) To study the cultures i.e. food habit, dress, religion, myths, beliefs, superstitions, music, dance, drama and literature of the two countries described in the travelogues;

ii) To examine various cultural issues and problems mentioned by the authors;

iii) To study special outlook in women's writing than their male counterparts;

iv) To make a comparative study of the books in respect of the different approaches of the authors.

Database and Methodology

It is a descriptive or analytical Paper. The use of literary tool and its geographical criticism is the major topic of discussion for the present study. The dichotomy to understand and narrate between the 'scientific' and 'literary' description of the respective places has been discussed from a view point of cultural Geography.

Culture and Cultural Space

Defining the word 'culture' is a complex and difficult task which has produced a range of very different definitions. Anthropologist Alfred Kroeber defined culture "Culture consists of pattern, explicit and implicit, of and for behavior acquired and transmitted by symbols constituting the distinctive achievements of human groups, including their embodiments in artifacts; the essential core of culture consists of traditional (i.e. historically derived and selected) ideas and especially their attached values..." (Kroeber & Kluckhohn, 1952). According to Robert M. Young, What is important about the concept of culture which is being developed and cultivated in cultural studies is that culture is seen as lived values or ways of life. This broadens and democratises culture and directs attention to subcultures, so that it embraces the culture of the home, neighbourhood, school, street corner, factory, disco, soap opera, pub, street market, prison, shopping mall, office, profession, seminar or study group, psychoanalytic or psychotherapeutic training institution, country club, college, bingo parlour, transport cafe, cinema, industry, motorway shop and petrol station, singles bar, gay bar, swimming pool, ghetto, motorcycle gang, gym, yoga class, women's or men's group - wherever people congregate and act in ways associated with particular activities, values and social relations (Robert M. Young, 1994).

Geographers divide geographical space in two types i.e. 'absolute space' and 'relative space'. Cultural space encompasses various components of material and social culture. It changes over time and place. Thus, cultural space is considered as relative space. In Bengali travel writings most of authors have narrated the story of people and culture of the exotic land. Sometimes their description is factual and extensive and sometimes it is superficial. But the writings of a woman have some specialty the perspective of her 'I' and 'eye'.

Sociologists divide culture in two kinds - material culture and non- material culture. A cultural region refers to an area over which the cultural traits of human groups may be identified. The culture and cultural environment of human groups (ethnic groups) vary

from place to place. This variation in cultural traits results into variation in human occupation and his organisation of space. A cultural region refers to an area over which the cultural traits of human groups may be identified. The culture and cultural environment of human groups (ethnic groups) varies from place to place. This variation in cultural traits results in variation in human occupation and his organisation of space.

Material Culture in Women's Writings

Material culture refers to the physical objects, resources, and spaces that people use to define their culture. These include homes, neighbourhoods, cities, schools, churches, synagogues, temples, mosques, offices, factories and plants, tools, means of production, goods and products, stores, and so forth. All of these physical aspects of a culture help to define its members' behaviours and perceptions. Material culture includes material or concrete things used by man such as house, household commodities, different kinds of apparatus, instruments, weapons, all of the physical objects that people create and give meaning to them.

Hariprava described the local culture wholeheartedly. She beheld fashionable buildings, pagodas and temples near Mountain Nikko. The sculptures were made of painted wood and copper. Here she found the priests of the temple wearing typical dresses termed as 'Boson'. (pp. 43-44)

We find the description of food, beverage and eating style of the common Japanese. Their style of eating is unique as they use two sticks at the time of eating. They neither use by milk to prepare any food nor they prepare sweetmeats. They prepare sweetmeat with rice or dal (made from pulses). 'Tofu' and 'Udon' are delicious vegetarian meal to the Japanese (p- 45).

Surprisingly, more than hundred years ago an ordinary Bengali women from Brahma society not only visited Japan with her Japanese husband but also narrated the educational system of the country. She got a chance of visiting a girls' school where Chemistry, Botany, Geology and general physiology would have been taught. In the colleges professional trainings like gardening, sewing, teaching music, crafting have been included with regular courses. The children would have been trained paper cutting, drawing etc. They also used to fabricate many earthen pots. Hariprava pointed out that the literacy rate was very high among male and female and it became possible due to the earnest effort on the part of government (pp.40-41).

Priti Sanyal describes the social culture as well as material culture of French community. She went a village to enjoy a festival of hunting birds. Except this, the readers come to know dress, fashion design, hair style, dance and other modes of entertainment (p. 19).

In Pere Lachaise cemetery she found the white marble statue of a lady overwhelmed with mourning. Raising two hands she is at prayer to God and her eyes are full of tears. The Statue appears as a symbol of melancholy (p. 53). The author visited Ramkrishna Mission known as 'Vedanta

Centre' which is situated at a small village thirty kilometer away from South-East of Paris (p. 86).

Non-material or Social Culture in Women's Writings

Non-material culture refers to the nonphysical ideas that people have about their culture, including beliefs, values, rules, norms, morals, language, organisations and institutions. For instance, the non-material cultural concept of religion consists of a set of ideas and beliefs in God, worship, morals, and ethics. These beliefs, then, determine how the culture responds to its religious topics, issues, and events.

While considering non-material culture, sociologists refer to several processes that a culture uses to shape its members' thoughts, feelings, and behaviours. Four of the most important of these are symbols, language, values, and norms. Non-material culture consists of thoughts and behaviour that people learn as part of the culture they live in. It includes abstract things, politics, economics, language, rules, customs, family, religion or beliefs, values, and knowledge.

At first, Hariprava reached Kobe station with her husband. She found various types of food like rice, 'Ocha' (tea), sweetmeat and milk were being sold in the stations. Rice and curry were sold in a small box and two bit of sticks tied up with ribbon would be given for eating rice. At that time, price of one box rice was fifty paisa (p. 35).

Hariprava became closely intimated with the social culture in her father-in-law's house within four months. As a common housewife she observed minutely the food habit of the Japanese. The cooking process of various cuisines was totally different from us. They give measured water in a an airtight pot for boiling rice and don't strain off water from it (it may be a pressure cooker). Without adding oil, ghee and spices they used to boil vegetable, fish and meat by 'Soio' (a kind of ill-smelling salty liquid). They eat half-boiled meat, uncooked and salted dry fish abundantly. Another favourite vegetable was radish. They keep it in a vessel by mixing salt and they take it after slightly being rotten (p- 45).

At that time she described their typical dress, religious belief and cultural activities. The people of the country used to put on wooden sandals called 'Gata'. She witnessed that the dresses of men and women are almost the same. 'Kimono' is a popular casual dress reaching down to the knees. A long and wide attractive ribbon which they use to tie up the Kimono is known as 'Obi'. The girth of women's Obi is slightly broader (than) the (men). In winter, they wear 'Howri' over Kimono which is extended almost to knee. The Japanese wear 'Tabi' (one type of socks made of white or black cloth which is elongated up to ankle). Besides their traditional dress, the author also found them with modern western dresses (pp. 47-48).

She visited Ise shrine, a famous pilgrimage with her husband. Before entering the shrine devotees had to take off their caps and ornaments. She went to a temple named 'Ten Gin- sama' (means departed souls) near Japanese port 'Moji'(p. 33). She has mentioned God 'Kami-sama' and other deities. It is interesting for the readers when she describes the ceremony of the Japanese (p. 50).

On New Year's Eve wearing new dress at night people go to the temple and offer 'Pronams' (prostration). On that day they decorate their rooms with colour paper and flags. Next day after bathing in the morning they start their daily activities. On an auspicious day they prepare cake and first offer it to their family deity and then the other members (p. 39).

While talking to each other the Japanese keep respect and courtesy. Wake up in the morning the children used to offer 'Morning Pronam' to their parents. They are famous for their hospitality and receive the guests cordially. Following their traditional culture they greet them and offer 'Ocha' (tea), biscuits and cake (p. 45).

At that time most of the Japanese were the follower of Buddhism and 'Shinto- Religion'. But some of the people would have followed Christianity. Hariprava found that traditional Buddhism was being changed. But she observed the influence of Shinto Religion above all. She mentioned 'Soknosa', a puja-festival remembering the dead heroes in many Buddhist and Shinto temples (p. 52).

Not with the eyes of a traveller but with eyes of a housewife Hariprava closely observed many affairs of Japanese society. During (her) staying in father-in-law's house for four months she got an opportunity to know the food, dress, marriage, religion, rituals, manners and customs of the Japanese. In this sense her travelogue is undoubtedly rich in social realities.

Talking about French life, Priti Sanyal cited that the French people lead a luxurious life. The record shows that (at least) one or two costly perfumes are regularly found in the monthly (shopping) list of eighty percent women (p. 13).

In her book she interestingly mentioned that the young generation (20-34 age group) who belong in middle class believe Astrology (p- 34). In religious life of the French the first day of November is known as 'Vhoo'. Except this, she talked about that French people also celebrate some festive like 'All Saint's Day', 'Remembrance Day' etc. When India celebrates Independence Day, in France Catholic religious festival "L'Assomption" is arranged (pp. 49, 79).

Modern art and amusement have been enlightened by Priti Sanyal. She visited the exhibition of Rene Lalique's achievement at Les Art Decoralif. She pointed out the trace of modern culture and politics on recent films. For example she told about famous Polish film-director Andrzej Wajda's long-awaited film 'Danton' (pp. 145 & 149).

She got a chance to go Book-fair in Paris. Here she found an interesting thing. The common people of France used to spend just twenty six minutes daily in reading books.

Among them most of the people spend their times by reading newspaper and various types of periodicals. But in 1985- 86 the number of new books published in France were 16200. Regarding this she has given a statistics of the preference of the books. According to her observation most of the people (almost fifty four percent) people are interested in reading novels particularly love-stories followed by history, memoirs, biography, autobiography etc. (pp. 173-176).

The author has narrated the culture and amusement of Bengali community in France. She attended 'Indian Festive' in Paris where two hundred fifty artists participated. The main theme of the festival was presenting rural Indian cultures such as folk-dances, folk-lore, folk-songs etc. In the festival a Bengali 'Baul' (wandering minstrel) was found passing through the gathering with 'Ektara' (a kind of one-string musical instrument) in his hand. Raghunath Goswami's doll-dancing stage gave the children much enjoyment. On the other hand, roundel dance of the artist from Madhya Pradesh, India was very attractive to the visitors. Manipuri-Dance and 'Tera Tali Dance' performed by the Rajasthani dancers had created a special charm also (pp. 198-200).

She gave a detailed account on expansion of Rabindra-Culture in France. The French edition of Rabindranath's 'Arupratan' (a drama) was first broadcasted from 'France Culture', a well-known Radio station on 24th December, 1990. Fifty actors and actress took part in the play. The drama was translated by fomous French actor Jacqueline Frederik Frie. The French title of this drama is 'Le Rai Ded La Chanbre Obscure'. It is actually the literary translation of Rabindranath's 'King of The Dark Chamber' (Bengali in original 'Raja'). The authors of France who helped to translate Rabindranath's literary works are Andre Gide, Mirabaud, Thorens, Jean Pierre and Jovan Except this, Kalidas Nag also translated 'Balaka' in French. The French people also (love) classical and folk-song (p- 230).

As an expatriate Bengali she noticed the expansion of Bengali culture in France. In a chapter of her book she only discussed the recent study on Rabindranath Tagore in France. She also wrote about the works of Sakti Burman, a contemporary Indian artist of Indian parentage living in France.

Crisis of society is a vital aspect in Priti Sanyal's writing. At the beginning of her writings she has given a statistics of the unmarried, widow and divorcees at that time. Live-together and open-relationship are the recent trend to the new generations. In spite of, the number of divorce is rapidly increasing (pp. 66-70).

She mentioned the (social) status of the immigrant community. It is a matter of great shock that in recent times antagonism has raised its head in France. Twenty percent of the total Asian emigrant population came from Vietnam, Cambodia and Laos as refugees. Notable that the refugees from South-East Asia have adjusted themselves with the original people of France. On the contrary, people mainly the Muslims from Algeria, Tunisia, Morocco and Middle-East Asia have not been received warmly (pp. 96-97).

If behind this antagonism lay only political or economic problems then its intensity could not be so acute. The actual problem behind this antagonism is cultural identity. The immigrated ones from North African countries lead a unique life which is completely different from the life of the western people. In this situation they are trying to create an enclave isolating themselves from the main stream (p. 99).

Difference from Male-authored Travelogues

How is women's travel writing different from men's? Such questions (are in..) danger of forcing all data into one or other of the gendered categories (such as language, subject-matter or narrational position), ignoring all material which can't be fitted into these categories. For the feminist critics, it is important to formulate more complex models of gender differences, in order to move away from a simple polarisation, towards a multi layered analysis where gender is sometimes the most salient feature in the production of a text and, at other times, is mediated through other factors.

Mills locates their narratives within larger structures of both material and symbolic power to stress the importance of the articulations of travel, gender and sexuality within travel culture: women paid attention to different things than men and had different expectations of themselves and of the 'natives' while abroad. In many contexts, accordingly, the similarities between male and female-authored travel accounts greatly outweigh any dissimilarities; and by the same token, there are few tendencies or characteristics in travel writing which are so uniquely feminine that they are never found in male-authored accounts. That said, factors (Foster and Mills, 2002). Foster and Mills also stress that within any given period and society one can usually detect broad patterns of difference between men's and women's travel writings (2002:4). And as Mills elsewhere points out, even men and women product more or less identical forms of travel writing, their travelogues will often be received very differently by the reading public, on account of the author's gender (Mills : 30). Thus a travel writer's gender may sometimes play a more important role in the reception, rather than the production, of a travel account.

Earlier it has been mentioned that 'Bangomohilar Japan Yatra' was the first Bengali travelogues on Japan. Thereafter Rabindranath Tagore wrote his famous travel account 'Japan Yatri' in 1916. After independence many travel accounts on Japan such as Annadasankar Roy's 'Japane' (1957), Bikash Biswas's 'Udito Bhanur Desh Japan'(1957), Narayan Sanyal's 'Japan Theke Fire' (1985) and Pabitra Sarkar's 'Japane Koyekdin' (1987) have been written. The authors have different backgrounds. They are either famous writers or travellers or academicians. They have narrated the story of physiography, society and culture of the said region but in most of the cases their descriptions are based on secondary information. Sometimes the authors are biased and their writings are 'unidirectional'. In this respect Hariprava Takeda's 'Bangomohilar Japan Yatra' is really exceptional piece. She told us the real story of the grassroots of Japan. We can't find such intensive description of the livelihood of the common people (specifically women and children) in male-authored travel accounts. Similarly, Asraf Siddiqi (*Paris Sundori*, 1957),

Nirod Mazumdar (*Punascho Pari*, 1988) and Sancu Maharaj (*Ek Farasi Nagore*, 1988) described mainly the scenic beauty, art, sculpture and cultural history of France. But Priti Sanyal in 'Farasi Desh Anyo Chokhey' consciously highlighted some problems and issues for the readers .

Comparison and Criticism

Though the books were written in different spatio-temporal context but some similarities are found here. Firstly, both of them have a positivistic view while depicting the facts. Secondly, in most of the Bengali travel accounts 'story of self' in exotic land occupies a major portion. But Hariprava Takeda and Priti Sanyal had no intention to propagate themselves. As Hariprava acquainted herself with Japanese family she had an opportunity to observe the society and culture of Japan very closely. She had created a 'relational space' in exotic land. Very consciously and carefully she observed the rituals, manners and customs. It is remarkable that she had no intention to compare the Japanese culture with her own culture (Bengali culture) and unnecessarily to establish the supremacy of own (as usually most of the Bengali authors do). Besides this we find out a nice description of dress, education and marriage in her writings. The critics comment that perhaps some of her explanations are not accurate but it must be acknowledged that in her travelogue there is no attempt to conceal the facts or to exaggerate that.

Priti Sanyal described her experiences in six chapters. She focused on changing mentality of young generation, fragile conjugal life, discriminations with minority communities and contemporary situation of the immigrants from Northern Africa. Lastly she described the expansion of Indian literature and art in French society. In spite of some similarities there are some dissimilarities also. Hariprava Takeda was an ordinary lady who married a Japanese man and visited Japan with her husband. She stayed there almost four months and deeply observed social and cultural life of common Japanese women. Her homely descriptions can easily attract any common reader. But it seems shallow to a reader who wants more detailing. On the contrary Priti Sanyal's writing is the blending of description and analysis. Its appeal is concentrated mainly to the sophisticated reader. Sometimes it is so 'literal' and 'abstract' that an ordinary reader may feel it uninteresting. While writing the preface of the book Sunil Gangopadhyay rightly said, it is neither a collection of essays nor an ideal travelogue... it is a blending of essay and belles-letters.

After all, the said travelogues are not above the criticism. Hariprava's writing is undoubtedly factual but few explanations she has given are not accurate. For example, she talked about 'Hara-kiri' (a ritual suicide by disembowelment with a sword, formerly practised in Japan by samurai) but the Japanese women never choose it to commit suicide. When she visited Japan (1912) there a political turmoil (Meiji Emperor died and Crown Prince Yoshihito succeeded to the throne as Emperor of Japan). But she didn't mention its impact on society. Priti Sanyal is staying in Paris for a long time but she doesn't able to create a 'relational space' with the locals. Lastly it can be said that the literary sensibilities have emerged a new academic interest in travel writings. Travel literature is always a blending of facts and fictions but when travel writings are not conducted under the sign of 'science' are virtually ignored.

Bibliography and References

Bande, U. (2003) *Cultural Space and Diaspora : Journey Metaphor in Indian Women's Writing,* Indian Institute of Advanced Study, Shimla, India

Blunt, A. & Rose, G. eds. (1995) *Writing women and Space: Colonial and Post-colonial Geographies,* Guilford Press, New York, USA

Blunt , Alison Mary. (1992) *Only A Women', Women Travel Writers and Imperialism,* The University of British Columbia, 1992

Clifford , James. (1992) *Travelling culture,* in Cultural Studies, Lawrence Gross-berg, Cary Nelson, and Paula A. Treichler, eds. London : Routledge, 1992

Crang, M. (1998) *Cultural Geography,* Routledge, London & New York,

Crang, M. (1998) *Self and other : Writing home, making territory and writing space,* Routledge, London and New York

Duncan, J. & , Gregory, D. (2002) *Writes of Passage: Reading Travel Writing,* Routledge, London and New York

Foster S., and Mills S. eds. (2002) *An Anthology of Women's Travel Writing,* Manchester University Press, USA

Kroeber, A.L., & Kluckhohn, C. (1952) *Culture: A critical review of concepts and definitions,* Harvard University Peabody Museum of American Archeology and Ethnology Papers 47

Renza, Louis A. *The Veto of the Imagination : A Theory of Autobiography* New Literary History 9 (1977): 1-26. Rpt. in Autobiography: Essays Theoretical and Critical. Ed. James Olney. Princeton: Princeton U P, 1980. (pp. 268-95).

Mills, S. (1993) *Discourses of Difference: An Analysis of Women's Travel Writing and Colonialism,* Routledge, New York, USA

Siegel. K edited (2004) *Gender, Genre & Identity in Women's Travel Writing* (p-193), Peter Long Publishing, Inc, New York, USA

Sultan, M.I, (2014) *Geographical 'Space' and Issues in Women's Writings: A Review of Two Bengali Travelogues,* International Journal of Innovative Research and Studies, vol. 3 issue 5 (pp. 713-725)

Sultan, M.I, (2016) *Appraisal of Geographical Realities in Bengali Travelogues on Foreign Countries in the Twentieth Century,* Ph.D Thesis (unpublished), Kolkata India

Thompson, C. (2011) *Travel Writing: The New Critical Idiom* London and New York Young, Robert M. (1994) *Mental Space* Process Press, UK

9

Women and Hinduism

Samahita Chawdhuri

Introduction

Since ancient times, the spirituality dominance over religious belief have transformed a lot and rise the present day modern religion. Such transformation has taken a long path. Since earlier days, religion and religious beliefs have been used for varieties of purposes like to maintain peace, to maintain injustice, while sometime to create unrest and political turmoil. Hence, people of dominant group used religious imagery to satisfy their needs over the weaker section of the society. Maintaining hierarchies of domination and oppression in different parts of the world in various ways, religions are playing active role. Not only that, institutionalised religions are also functioned to alleviate sufferings caused by these very hierarchies of domination and suppression.

Religion

According to Roland Robertson, "religion refers to the existence of supernatural beings, which have a governing effect on life". Melford E. Spiro describes religion is based on "beliefs in superhuman beings and in their power to assist or harm man." Hence all definitions of religion emphasize certain characteristics while exclude others. In both the definitions of Spiro and Robertson, they focussed on the nature of religious beliefs.

Origin of Religion-

From earlier days, we can identify some perspectives which through light on the evolution of religion. These are-

i) Evolutionary Perspective, which try to solve questions like 'how did religion begin' or how did religion evolve?' In its inception days, this approach was influenced by Charles Darwin through his influential work 'on the Origin of Species'. Like Darwin's 'Origin of Species', wherehe mentioned his evolutionary approach regarding evolution of species, so social scientists tried to explain the evolution of religion. Under this evolutionary approach, two main theories are important which are animism and naturism. Animism, as per the viewsof Edward B. Tylor, depends on the idea of spirit and religion originated in order to satisfy the intellectual nature of human being and making sense of death, dream and visions. The second theory is Naturism. Influenced by the views of F. Max Muller, this theory believes in supernatural power. In other words, naturism is individual'sresponse to the effect of the power and wonder of nature which control individual's emotions.

ii) Functionalist Perspectives- It involves the analysis, which is primarily concerned with the contribution that religion makes to fulfil the functional requirements of society. Among all functionalist theories, most influential interpretation is 'The Elementary Forms of the Religious Life' by Emile Durkheim. Durkheim argues that, religion occupies the 'sacred' part of the society, which is set apart of the un-sacred portion. Sacred thing are mainly symbols which represents beliefs and practices of members of the society. According to him, 'collective conscience', i.e., shared values and moral beliefs play vital role in social life. Collective worship is another group activity emphasized by Durkheim, which strengthen the society.

Bronislaw Malinowski, unlike Durkheim, identified particular areas of social life with, which religion is concerned like anxiety, emotion, tension etc. Talcott Persons, like Malinowski, related religion to particular problems of all societies. He categorise these problems under two headings. One is those sudden events for, which people cannot prepare themselves like the events of premature death. The second problem is 'uncertainity', i.e., the endeavour in which a great deal of effort have been applied but unknown the result. For example, the prediction of weather upon agriculture.

iii) Marxian Perspective- According to Marx, religion is an illusion and does not have any capacity to solve society's or human's problem. In Marxian perspective, most religious movements originate in oppressed classes. Not only that, ruling classes also adopt religious beliefs to justify their position both to themselves and to others. According to Marxian perspective, religion acts as a mechanism of social control, which maintains the existing systems of class relationship.

Many feminist writes are dissatisfied with Marxian theory. According to them, this theory fails to provide a proper explanation for gender inequality. Shulasmith Firestone, in her book, "The Dialectic of Sex" mentioned that, gender division in labour is more basic than the specialized division of labour, which differentiates all members of society and the economic class system where division is done among men and women population. As women bore children, thus they have to depend on men for survival. Such a dependency on men create unequal power relationships and it subsequently develop into gender-biased socio-economic stratification system.

Gender Role in Religion

The controversial custom ofbanning female entry to the Sabarimala temple, Kerala is an example of gender inequality in religious institutions. There is a custom of restricting female entry (particularly females of age 10-50, i.e., mainly reproductive age females) to the Sabarimala temple, which is believed could vitiate the strict celibacy practised by the presiding deity, Ayyappa (The Telegraph, 14th October, 2017). Actually, overall gender equality in social institutions all over the globe are recorded under strict consideration; but gender equality in religious sphere usually creates controversies and social unrest. Some temples restrict women's entry near to the deity irrespective of the gender of the deity. Thus religion may be considered as one of the most potential way of expressing one's through liberating spirituality; but some peculiar avenues of gendered interpretations and practices are entertained by every religion to restrict free movement of women in this religious sphere of life. Revised interpretations are required to release patriarchy's religious stranglehold and open the door of all religious institutions equally to both males and females.

O'Neil, Bilgin and Lan in their paper 'The effects of religious beliefs on the working decisions of women: Some evidence from Turkey' examine the decision taken by Turkish women regarding their participation in labour force. They found that, religious belief, rituals and regular practices have greatest negative effect on women's participation in labour force not for uneducated but also for educated women, who are the most productive human resource in the economy. According to the authors, there are number of factors affecting low female work participation rate in Turkey.

Among them, the religious factors are crucial.

Carol Ann Drogus mentioned in the article 'Religious Change &Womens' Status in Latin America' that religion has played a significant role in Latin American culture including shaping concepts on beliefs about gender. Changes in beliefs and opportunities within a particular religion, may affect strongly regarding womens' participation in labour force. This paper examines that Latin America's culture including gender roles are deeply rooted in Mediterranean culture.

C. Derichs and A. Fleschenberg in their edited book 'Religious fundamentalism and their gendered impacts in Asia' state that the stereotypical assignation of gender roles actually limit the space for diversity especially the socio-political participation of women which subsequently leads to erosion of the democratic pility and respect for human rights. This volume concentrates o South and South-east Asia and examines the impact of religiously inspired policies on the female population in Sri Lanka, the Philippines, Indonesia and Malayasia.

M. F. Bednarowski in her paper 'Outside the Mainstream: Women's Religion and Women Religious Leaders in 19th century America' states that, to understand the status of women in a particular religious tradition, one has to consider four topics within that tradition- the character of the divine, human nature, function of the clergy and the nature of marriage.

Loewenthal, MacLeod and Cinnirella mentioned in their paper "Are women more religious than men? Gender differences in religious activity among different religious groups in the UK" mentioned that, by examining four religious- cultural groups in the UK that, who are more religious- men or women completely depend on culture. Many religious traditions differentiate between the religious obligations of men and women and place a particular half of the population (either men or women) to fulfil religious duties. But men play more vital role as priests in each and every religious belief. Traditional Judaism and Islam place less important role to women than on men and more effective role to the traditional allocation of primary homemaking and child-care responsibilities to women.

Women in Hinduism

Hinduism is the oldest ofall the major religions of the world, which dates back to 4500 years ao for its origin. Majority of followers are in India. The Vedas and the Upanishadas, the oldest Hindu scriptures depicted the images of women in many ways. Some times, they are depicted as images of selfishness, energy and ambition when these women neglect to serve the family for their higher levels of womanhood. Women are also depicted as loving saints and also as violent ogresses. These varieties of images of women one can find in Hindu epics (Ramayana and Mahabharatas), in the Hindu scriptures (the Vedas, The Upanishadas). In reality, the Hindu ideal is gender balanced with man as the creator and women as the lover. Hindus celebrate a number of female goddesses, saints and deities, who are worshiped as a symbol of fertility, creation and hope. "Hinduism has the longest-continuing goddessheritage in the world and offers models for men and women to follow and revere" (Lyndey, 2011:340). Women lead in religious rituals at home and in temples.

Maa Laxmi

Maa Kali

In Hinduism, women's role are more dominant in domestic sphere as homemakers, wives and mothers. In many cases, Hindu goddesses are worshiped to secure lives of men. For example, Goddess Laxmi is worshiped for the benefit of male members of the family who earn money for the livelihood. Thus, Laxmi is worshipped in every shop asshe is the Goddess of wealth. On the other hand, hindu scriptures tell us that, Ma Kali, when became very much angry, her husband Lord Mahadev lay down on ground to stop her. Here we can see several images of women in Hinduism. In another case, goddess Durga took birth from various parts ofthree male deities- Brahma, Vishnu and Maheswar. They created Devi Durga to stop the destruction caused by another male villain 'Asura' and save the whole universe. Instead of creating a God, they have created a female to save the universe.

Devi Durga

Conclusion

Based on archaeological evidence of historic and pre-historic societies, researchers identified a glimpse of first civilization as exhibiting gynocentrism, meaning emphasis on female and feminine interests. The term originates from two words, 'Gyno' meaning woman and 'Centron' meaning centre. Gynocentrism is a radical feminist concept which highlights female consciousness, cultural as well as social awareness caused by women-centred beliefs, identity crisis and so on. Not only that, it challenges androcentric consciousness of masculine standard. In androcentric perspective masculine activities are projected as normative and androcentric believes of females presented as deficient and secondary, which subsequently has transformed to the gynocentric positive thinking regarding females. Elaine Showalter is one of the first feminists to develop a systematic programme to illuminate the culture of women writers and readers, which is developed as a critical analysis of androcentrism.Though androcentrism refers to patriarchy but in some ancient societies, gynocentrism refers to partnership and not to matriarchy. The terms, patriarchy and matriarchy refer to a ranking of one part of humanity over the other while the term partnership is based on the principle of linking rather dominance or separateness. In Hinduism, one can find a number of both male and female deities, saints who are worshiped by all members of society irrespective of their gender.

References

Drogus,Carol Ann. 1994. 'Religious Change And Women's Status In Latin America', Working paper- 205. The Helen Kelogg Institute for International Studies

Haralambos, M. and R. M. Heald. 2010. Sociology: Themes and Perspectives.Oxford University Press, New Delhi

Kate Miriam Loewenthal, Andrew K Mac LeodMarco Cinnirella 2002. 'Are women more religious than men? Gender differences in religious activity among different religious groups in the UK' in Personality and Individual differences, Vol 32 Issue 1.

Lewis, James R. Scientology. 2009. Oxford Univ Press, New York

Mallinowski, B. 1954.Magic, Science and Religion and Other Essays. Anchor Books, New York

Robertson, R. 1970. The Sociology of Religion.Penguin Books, Harmondsworth.

Stuart, Alison 2010. 'Freedomof Religion andGender Equality: Inclusive orExclusive?' in Human Rights Law Review 10:3 Published by Oxford University Press.

Williams, Catharina P. 2008. 'Female transnational migration, religion and subjectivity: The case of Indonesian domestic workers' in Asia Pacific Viewpoint, Vol. 49, No. 3, December 2008 (344–353)

Web link

https://www.jnu.ac.in/Faculty/maitrayee/Feminism%20in%20Print%20Media.pdf

http://dspace.nehu.ac.in/bitstream/1/7647/3/Indian%20woman%20(M%20Renganathan).pdf

https://lib.ugent.be/fulltxt/RUG01/000/742/862/RUG01-000742862_2010_0001_AC.pdf

http://shodhganga.inflibnet.ac.in/bitstream/10603/50813/8/08_chapter%20i.pdf

https://takku.net/mediagallery/mediaobjects/orig/f/f_val-plumwood-feminism-and-the-mastery-of-nature-pdf.pdf

10

Women in Vedic Period

Bratati Dey

Introduction

India has an ancient history of more than 4000 years. The views on status of women are reflected in the Vedas, Upanishads, the Manudharma Sastra, the Arthasastra of Kautilya, by Ramayana and Mahabharatha, Purana and other writings of the Indian culture and thinking.

Women in India, like in many other societies, have passed through a turbulent range of social transformation and upheavals, historical phases and political struggles. Present study tries to focus on the status of women in Vedic age in early India. It is believed that women enjoyed a very high and equal status in the early Vedic, Vedic or in ancient India. There are contrasting views. Nevertheless, it on this; nevertheless, what is upheld by many thinkers is that women in those days did not suffer from much indignity and oppression. Ancient Indian Grammarians such as Patanjali1 and Katyayana have illustrated this. It is also stated that much before the commencement of the civilization, matriarchy was very much in vogue across many parts of India.

Feminist Theoretical Perspective

Historical literatures are very significant evidences for societal study. Vedic period literatures are the valuable sources of study of women status in society. Feminist theories try to open up this lance according to time and location. In the second half of the twentieth century, feminism emerged as the most powerful movement that almost swept the literary world. It has been articulated differently in different parts of the world including India, by different people especially women depending upon their class, background and level of consciousness. Initially, in the western countries, women revolted to fight for emancipation and liberation from all forms of oppression by the state, by society and by men. This paper tries to focuses on the women status in society, rather than nature of work it's find out their cultural inclusion in society.

Cultural feminists believe that the cause of women's oppression is biological. Their body is the material base of reproduction of human beings. It is natural procreative mechanism; its sexuality is controlled by men through the institutions of marriage and family. The male culture dominates and oppresses women in socio-economic field. These feminists are committed to change the patriarchal system which is the root cause of many social problems. To study the Vedic period this backdrop sense very necessary for critical study.

Some feminists most notably Alice Echols and Ellen Willis, hold that after about 1975 most of what continued to be called "radical feminism" represents a narrow subset of what was originally a more ideologically diverse movement. Echols labels this dominant tendency–"Cultural Feminism" and "view it as a neo Victorian ideology coming out of radical feminism but ultimately antithetical to it." She says, "Whereas the original radical feminism challenge the polarization of the sexes, cultural feminism simply embraces the positive feminine virtues."

Cultural feminism commends the positive aspects of what is seen as the female character or feminine personality. It is also a feminist theory that praises the positive aspect of women. Early theorists like Jane Addams and Charlotte

Perkins Gilman argue that in governing the state, cooperation, caring and non violence in the settlement of conflicts society seem to be what is needed from women's virtues. They believe in equal partnership of men and women who have separate existence and different basic functions. This is very significant for the study of Vedic women and their status in society.

Status of Women in Society

During the time of the Rg-Veda, woman was a symbol of strength (Shaksthi) and generosity. She had a share in property as a daughter and the freedom to choose her husband. The bride used to be blessed to be the 'Empress to one's father-in-law and mother-in-law; to the sisters-in-law and brothers-in-law; speak to all in the family with power and authority, be kind to both the two feet and four feet animals'. Thus, the status of a wife was very high during the Rg Vedic times.

During the pre-vedic age, it is believed that Dravidian culture was more popular in practice. The scholars who have studied the religious aspects of Sindhu culture have felt that it had some of the earliest fossils relating to the status of women. Idols of pregnant women, women wearing head gear etc., imply that women were treated with a lot of honour during this time. The reproductive function of women was held in high esteem. They came to be worshipped as denoting the entire universe.

It is also stated that women in the Rg Vedic period were very close to men in terms of holding power and authority. The entire management of the household was in their hands. Woman was the head of the household. All servants, finances, livestock were in her hands only. She used to take care that the fire in the Yagna never gets extinguished; got educated like her brothers, learnt the use of arms, warfare etc (like her brothers); participated in Yaga-Yagnas (like her husband) and took part in warfare, ran behind enemies;

whatever she used to do during childhood, like milking the cow, cleaning the food grains, knitting and embroidery, filling water – all these will be forgotten later when she gets into the duties of a wife. Now, she gets into familial and social roles; shuns the veil (purdah) and openly shows her face while participating in religious activities. She also takes part in warfare and demonstrates her courage and valour; undertakes many Yaga-Yagnas, like the male saints did.

Women were saints and poetesses too. They have authored many 'Mantras' (chanting) of the Rg-Veda. The Aryan women used to recite the Mantras with equal devotion and respect as they did while reciting the Mantras written by the male saints. There are examples of women sages, like Apala, Ghosha, Vishwavara, Lopamudra, Shachi-Poulami, and Vagumbhruni and so on. These names are reflected in the Rg Veda, along with the Mantras they recited. Vagumbhruni is noted for the blessings she gives to all the 10 directions – 'I will support by being Rudra's (Shiva's) arrow in his bow to kill those who hate Lord Brahma and will bring the Sun into the solar system to do good to all the people'.

Shachi-Poulami, another woman sage, says 'Just as the sun rises to the centre of the sky, even my luck is going high; the other wives of my husband are destroyed; my sons have become rulers of the ten directions, my husband Indra has obtained his strength by virtue of the worship and prayers that I have undertaken'.

These illustrations show that women in ancient India were supposed to enjoy equal status with men in all walks of life. They received good education. There were no child marriages and women married at an adult age, freely selecting their husband. As noted already, there were several sages among women like Maitreyi, Lopamudra and Gargi.

Dharmasastras of Apastamba (450 – 350 BCE) speak about womanly behavior and state that women are enjoined to be of service to their husbands. There were also kingdoms that boasted of a Nagarvadhu, who was the most beautiful woman. She was respected as a goddess but was treated as a courtesan. It is argued that it was polygyny and the practice of having many wives that led to the downfall of women's status.

Role of Women in Society

It has been observed that dharmasastra has significant role to controlling social life in ancient Vedic age. Thus, 'dharma' is what is firm and durable, what sustains and maintains, what hinders fainting and falling. The word appears to be used in the same sense in a few of the passages of the ancient-most documents of Vedic language.[1] Though the Vedas are counted as the foremost among the sources of dharma, they do not profess to be formal treatises on dharma; they only contain disconnected statements on the various aspects of dharma. The Vedas are considered as sruti, i.e. revelation, while the smriti, i.e. tradition is the second important sources of dharma. Smriti comprises of the six vedangas, the epics and the Puranas. Rules of dharma are contained in all these works.[2] Thus originally it seems that most of the dharmasutras were attached to a particular Vedic school. The dharma-sutras bear a close relation to the grhya-sutras in all respects. The connection is not only linguistic but also as regards the subject matter. In these regards role of women in Vedic age is very significant. It has been observed that the dharma-sutras contain rules about the samskaras, including marriage, on the asramas, including the duties of men and women, the householder, on funeral oblations etc. But they seldom describe the rituals of domestic life; they touch upon it only in passing.

During the period of Veda the household controlled by the patriarch, the grhapati, is recognized as the central institution in the dharmasastra as well as the dharmasutras. In the Gruhya Sutras, the Samskaras of people compulsorily had to be done. The religious and bodily samskaras that are carried out to a man from birth to death numbering 40 are explained in terms of their nature, process etc. All the Samskaras had to take place for the men with the chanting of Mantras, Mantropadesha, Upanayana, Veda studies, marriage etc. Samskaras of Ashrama life became associated with the man and his personality development. All should happen to him, but for the women, only marriage had to be conducted to the chanting of Mantras. All other Samskaras can be without Mantras like Jataka in childhood, naming ceremony, Choodakarma etc., without any Mantras. Even during the times of marriage, the purohit can speak for her. Although she was called as Yagnopaveethini, no thread was used. Only a small cloth was put on her waist from left to right.

Macdonell says that the Smrithis framed and designed the wider range of rules and regulations of Dharmasastras. Their interpretation of the lives of women is more in terms of societal than religious. They have tried to keep women away from religion as far as possible. Manu, Baudhyayana, Gauthama, Parashara, Yajnavalkya, Vishnu, Narada and others' Dharma Sutras helped in framing the life and religious system of Hindu society. Their interpretation, commentary and policies are practiced even to this day. Mithakshari was written as a critique of Yagnavalkya Smritis and Medathithi against Manusmrithi, Manu, Baudhyayana and Yagnavalkya have not allowed entry for women in religious sphere. The very existence or birth of women according to them is to beget progeny.

Manu is important among Dharmasutrakaras. He is a great social reformer/organizer. He has identified the role of women in organizing a systematic society, because, he has specific ideas about women's religious roles. First of all, Manu thinks of a woman as one who does not deserve any freedom. All her Dharmic achievements, philanthropy, freedom are irrelevant as her nature is just opposite to theirs. But he felt that all the Samskaras of men need to happen to women too and with Mantras – according to Manu. Marriage itself is upanayana to a woman. Serving husband is a life of learning to her. Agni parikriya is household work. Vivaha is upanayana and there is no need for any separate knowledge, japa, thapa, puja or home for her independently. By serving her husband well, she gets everything to herself too. Women should not conduct Yagnas and even if they did, Brahmins should not attend them. Like a spinster even a widow can perform them and attain moksha.

Thus, Manu placed women in the circle of religious practices, marriage, serving one's husband, begetting sons etc. The Dharma Sutrakaras did not prescribe Vairagya to women. Sanyasa is not for her according to them.

Conclusion

In the opinion of the historians, the Rg-Vedic times were the early rising of the civilization. The religious practices and ideals were simple and beautiful at that time. In the Rgveda, there is mention about a number of Brahmavadinis. There are a number of illustrations of how women scholars like Gargi and Maithreyi who tackled sage Yagnavalkya with their knowledge on Vedas.

In the beginning, the woman was managing yagnas independently. Being alone, unmarried, Vedhadhyayana, Yagna Sadhana were undertaken by her. She sang the Samas, washed the sacrificial animal, arranged the Yagna Peetha etc, but these were carried out without any distinction as male or female. However, as Yagna came to be a samsthe in the Brahmanas, it became more complex. Rules, regulations, modes of carrying out all became immense in number. The process of Yagna became distributed amongst many and as division of labour came about, even people were distributed as doing different types of work. Groups were formed to do such work. Hotru, Adhvaryu, Udgathru, Brahman, Ruthvija, Purohit, etc., were engaged in developing Yagnas, Karma Kandas, etc. Unfortunately, more than the moral intention of Yagnas, external practices came to be given more importance. Thus, instead of being a means of pleasing gods, it became a means of seeking whatever the people wanted to get/possess. Thus, in the Brahmanas, Dharma Sadhana crossed the limits of individual and family life and came to the inevitable stage of collective co-operation. This pushed women more and more towards the family and household work. All her religious activities became relevant to be carried out by different groups. Even her own rights as a wife to perform Yagnas became restricted and her identity was namesake and further came to be represented only by symbolic things. In the Rg Vedas, we get two types of information about women. One, that they were called as Brahmavadinis and two, as Sadhyavadhus. The Sadhyavadhus were those who did Vedadhyayana in childhood and in youth as far as possible, and got married after they attained puberty. The Rg Veda addressed them as the river which is going to join the sea.

Brahmavadinis were those who remained unmarried for a long time engaged in Vedadhyayana. They used to have Upanayana and other samskaras and participated in daily rituals. They conducted Yagnas, Yagas, rituals and understood and mastered over the meaning of Vedas, also had evinced interest in such Darshanas as Purva Meemamsa; used to bring about reform in religious sector too. Bruhat Devata gives a list of Brahmavadinis. Saamaveda has called Noida, Akrustabhasha, Sikathanivavari, Uttaratchvika, Goupyayana as Rushikas. Lopamudra, Vishwavara, Ghosha are called as Brahmavadinis. There were both married and unmarried among them. Marriage was not a compulsion before Brahmavadinis.

Gargi, Maithreyi, Kathyayini, Sulabha, Vadaba, Prachdeya, representing their times in the above scholarship and who were proficient in Vedic studies, participated in seminars like true scholars.

In the Vedic Age, some Yagnas used to be meant exclusively to be performed by women. Seethayagna, Rudrayagna, Rudra Bali etc., are examples here. Seethayagna was performed by women to beget good harvest. Women used to pray to Rudra through Rudra yagna for their Soubhagya. Rudrabali was given to protect the livestock. Women used to join men in performing Somayagna.

We have seen that two schools of thought have co-existed in Indian understanding of the status of women. One considered women as 'equal to men'; the other holds them as objects of hatred. Both arguments have drawn heavily upon ancient scripts and passages from religious literature to prove that women are so (equal to men or as someone to be hated). For example, Apastamba prescribed that 'All must make a way for a woman when she is treading a path'. This was taken to mean a mark of respect to woman as usually such behaviour indicates showing respect to someone who is very respectable. Manu also held similar views on women, showing utmost respect and honour. He is quoted to be saying that 'where the female relations live in grief, the family soon wholly perishes; but where they are not unhappy, the family ever prospers'. Manu also went to say that 'where women are honoured, the gods are pleased but where they are not honoured no sacred rite yields any reward'. Yagnavalkya had said, ' women are the embodiment of all divine virtues on earth'; for example, Soma bestowed all his purity on them; Gandharva has given them sweetness of speech and fire has showered all his brilliance to make them most attractive'.

The epics Ramayana and Mahabharatha also present statements about lofty ideals of womenhood. The latter considered women as the pillars of social organization and centres of domestic life. It also held that a man is inferior to a woman before whom he should bend his will. He should serve and adore her.

References:

1. Allchin, B and Allchin R (1968), The Birth of Indian Civilization: India and Pakistan before 500 B.C, Penguin books, Baltimore.
2. Altekar, A.S (1987), The Position of Women in the Hindu Civilization, 2nd ed., Motilal Banarsidas, Delhi.
3. Banerjee, Sures Chandra (1962), Dharmasastras: A Study in their Origin and Development, Punthi Pustak, Calcutta.
4. Chandra Vinita (2010), *Gender Relations in Early India,* Rawat Publication, India.
5. "The World Book Encyclopedia", Vol. 7, (London Sydney: World Book International, Rpt, 1992), p. 49
6. Ibid, p.49
7. R.K. Dhawan, "Feminism and Recent Indian Literature", (Prestige, New Delhi, 2008) p.9
8. Retrieved from 'http:/wikipedia.org/wiki/"radical feminism".
9. Ibid.
10. R.K. Dhawan, "Feminism and Recent Indian Literature", (Prestige, New Delhi, 2008) p.20
11. Retrieved from "http:/Wikipedia.org/wiki/cultural feminism".
12. Simone De Beauvoir, "The Second Sex" (The New English Library, London, 1966) p.155. 64
13. Dr. S. Radhakrishnan, 'Fundamental Unity - Women in Indian Culture', (From Jain Study Circular, October 1983).
14. Retrieved from http/en.wikipedia.org/wiki/Feminism In India
15. Manjushree (1990), *Position of Women in the 'Yajnavalkyasmrti',* Prachi Publishes, New Delhi, India.
16. Mahatma Gandhi, 'Equal in Status- Women in Indian Culture', (From Jain Study Circular, October 1983).
17. Swami Vivekananda, 'Women of India' Reports in American Newspapers, (Detroit Free Press, March 25, 1894) Vol. III.

About the Contributors

1. **Taruna Bansal and Awadh Narayan Choubey**

Dr. Taruna Bansal has a diverse work experience spanning urban geography and gender studies. An alumnus from Jawaharlal Nehru University she completed her doctoral studies from the Centre for the Study of Regional Development, Jawaharlal Nehru University. She joined the Department of Geography, Faculty of Natural Sciences, Jamia Millia Islamia, New Delhi as a Lecturer in 2006 and has been with it ever since in the capacity of Assistant Professor.

She has published two books and ten research papers in various refereed journals, conference proceedings and edited books. She has presented a large number of research papers in different seminars, workshops and conferences held in different parts of the country as well as in University of Hong Kong and University of Nottingham. She is an executive member of Indian National Cartographic Association (INCA). She is also a life member of Society for Urban Ecology (SURE) and Association of Punjab Geographers (APG).

Her research interests include urban studies with emphasis on ecological and historical perspectives and gender studies, highlighting the role of women in the society and economy. She has also been working on different cartographic, remote sensing and GIS Techniques and their applications in geography.

Awadh Narayan Choubey is a research scholar of the Department of Geography, Jamia Millia Islamia, New Delhi, India.

2. Arundhati Bhattacharyya

Dr Arundhati Bhattacharyya is working as an Assistant Professor, Department of Political Science, Diamond Harbour Women's University in West Bengal. She is an alumnus of Presidency College, Kolkata and Jawaharlal Nehru University. Her areas of specialisation are gender and International Relations. She has presented papers in national and international seminars in India and abroad. She has written 3 books and has contributed to national and international publications. She has completed UGC and ICSSR projects. She is a resource person of MHRD. She had been invited by CEDAW, United Nations as an oral speaker on Rural Women.

3. Nirupama Patwardhan

She is a Ph.D. Scholar in Symbiosis International University (SIU) doing her thesis under the supervision of **Prof. Shubhasheesh Bhattacharya. Dr. Shubhasheesh Bhattacharya is** Professor & HOD – HR, Symbiosis Institute of International Business (**SIIB**), (Symbiosis International University)

4. Shelly De Pandit

Shelly De (Pandit) is an Assistant Professor of Commerce in Bijoy Krishna Girls' College, Howrah in West Bengal. She has completed her Minor Research Project under UGC and written various research papers on relevant issues. She has presented papers in national and international seminars in India and contributed to national and international publications.

5. Saswati Ghosh

Saswati Ghosh holds an M Phil (CU) and a Doctorate Degree (JU) in Economics. She teaches Economics to

Honours and General students in City College (Main) — affiliated to University of Calcutta, as a full-time UGC teacher, now as the HOD, as an Associate Professor. She also has taught Economics and gender at various levels, including M Phil in Economics (CU) and Women's Studies (JU), served as advisor to many projects including one funded by EU. Saswati's specialization in Quantitative Techniques helps her to measure quality of life, role of the state vis-à-vis gender, tribal women. She writes regularly in various dailies and journals and is a known columnist, raising difficult questions. She has three Bengali books on the topics of gender and economics, theory and practice of the women's movement, and an activist guide to the Domestic Violence Act. Her contributions have been included, both in English and Bengali, in many academic and popular compilations.

6. **Shreya Mukherjee**

Shreya has completed graduation and post-graduation in History of Art from Visva-Bharati. In 2004 she joined as a lecturer of art history in College of Art and Design Burdwan till 2014. At present she is pursuing research on 'History of Indian photography', from the department of Art History, Kala- Bhavana Visva Bharati

7. **Lopamudra Maitra Bajpai**

Dr. Lopamudra Maitra Bajpai is a Culture Specialist and working as an Indian representative-South Asian Association for Regional Co-operation- Cultural Centre, Colombo, Sri Lanka. She is an alumnus of Presidency College, Kolkata and Deccan College, Pune. She is a Visual Anthropologist and got her MA, MDMC, PhD from Indian Council for Historical Research- JRF- Govt. of India. She has presented papers in national and international seminars in India, abroad and contributed to national and international publications.

8. Md Iqbal Sultan

Dr Md. Iqbal Sultan, Assistant Professor, Department of Geography, Gokhale Memorial Girls' College, Kolkata. He is especially interested in Social, Cultural, Political and Tourism Geography. Dr Sultan has completed his research on Bengali travelogues from Calcutta University. His Ph.D thesis was *Appraisal of Geographical Realities in Bengali Travelogues on Foreign Countries in The Twentieth Century*. Some articles have been published in national and international journals. He also published a book on Geographical Field Study.

9. Samahita Chawdhuri

Dr. Samahita Chowdhury is an Assistant Professor in Geography in Bijoy Krishna Girls' College, Howrah in West Bengal. She has written various research papers on relevant issues. She has presented papers in national and international seminars in India and contributed to national and international publications.

10. Bratati Dey (Ed.)

Bratati Dey, Assistant Professor and Head of the Department of Geography in Dhruba Chand Halder College, South 24 Parganas, West Bengal. Completed project (UGC funded) on Gender studies. She has participated national and international conferences and seminars for research presentation.

Index